Broken I Am Free

Kaela Saner

TRILOGY

Broken I Am Free

Trilogy Christian Publishers A Wholly Owned Subsidary of Trinity Broadcasting Network

2442 Michelle Drive Tustin, CA 92780

Cover design by: Natalee Dunning

For information about special discounts for bulk purchases, please contact Trilogy Christian Publishing.

Manufactured in the United States of America

10 9 8 7 6 5 4 3 2 1

Library of Congress Cataloging-in-Publication Data is available.

ISBN: 978-1-68556-192-5
E-ISBN: 978-1-68556-193-2

To my mom and grandma, thank you for picking up the pieces
of my broken heart.
Thank you for drying my tears and the warm hugs.
I love you both very much.

TABLE OF CONTENTS

Introduction...vii

Section 1: Brokenness...1

    Chapter 1: The Heart of Us 3

    Chapter 2: Broken by Others...........................11

    Chapter 3: A Broken World.............................27

Section 2: Proud Heart...41

    Chapter 4: Our Downfall 43

    Chapter 5: Surrender 59

Section 3: Forgive...71

    Chapter 6: Scars..73

    Chapter 7: Cracks...85

    Chapter 8: Filled...101

Section 4: Healing 109

    Chapter 9: Open Heart 111

    Chapter 10: Faith in Healing 119

Section 5: Redemption 135

    Chapter 11: Redeemed Heart 137

    Chapter 12: A Forever Heart 151

Endnotes 161

About the Author 165

INTRODUCTION

When I was in the depths of studying and researching Scripture for this book, fear started to settle within my heart, fear of sharing my story, fear of being vulnerable, and fear of what others might think. This was a fear that caught my breath, made my heart beat double out of my chest, and shot anxiety all through my body. It was a fear that made me want to retreat and cower. To stay in the confines of my utopia bubble and to hide everything away that could hurt me.

This fear of sharing my story constricted my throat. I didn't want to revisit that pain, that brokenness. No. Wait. I'm not being honest with myself. I didn't want others to know my pain and brokenness—especially the ones who caused the heartbreak. I didn't want them to know how much they hurt me and how weak I felt in the presence of the pain. I didn't want them to know the sadness, the anger, the bitterness, and the hate that took over my being. I didn't want to get in a vulnerable state that left me open to another calculated attack flaying open my heart again, letting it bleed the life away to where there would be no coming back from the brink of darkness.

As I am writing this, my mind goes towards this pain, a pain that was a dark, fearful hole. Yet, the fear that coursed through me was just a brief few seconds. But in those seconds, I saw clarity, and I felt a wholesome peace. I saw God in my pain. I saw Him in my brokenness. Though I did have a part in the cause of my hurts, He was still ever there. He was in every facet. He has to be in every facet because without Him, I would not be here today writing this. Without Him, I wouldn't be able to comprehend my pain, let alone heal from my pain. God is solely at the heart of all that I am. He is my rescuer, and He is the focal point of overcoming brokenness. He is in all the brokenness.

Though my story will be told throughout this book, it is just a small part of brokenness throughout the world. Brokenness is found everywhere you look. You see it in the broken smile and saddened eyes of people that pass you by on the sidewalk. You see it in the countless shootings or the millions of girls, boys, women, and men caught in the multi-million dollar industry of modern-day slavery (human trafficking). It is everywhere. It is devastating to the heart and soul that God meant for an everlasting life of happiness and joy. A heart and soul He meant for laughter, smiles, snuggles, cuddles, and togetherness.

This journey of brokenness is divided up into five sections: brokenness, a prideful heart, forgiveness, healing, and redemption. Each scripture that is at the beginning of every chapter will be applied to brokenness in some way or form. I wrote this book for those who feel like they are broken or know someone that is. The journey I will take you on is from having a broken heart to having a redeemed heart. It requires great courage to delve back into your brokenness and a strength that only God can give. But I assure you whenever God opens your mind, eyes, and heart to you; you will discover that you are not a broken mirror, and your heart is not shattered into a million pieces. You have a Healer on your side, and He is the Redeemer of your heart and soul. Though the pain, the bruises, and the hurts may be unbearable at times and hard to comprehend, let alone see the next step in front of you,

God did not make you an image of this world. He made you an image of Himself. Indeed, you are not broken fully. You are just merely bent with some cracks. But those same cracks and that same bent will be put to right with the healing and redemption of God. Trust Him in this journey and give over all your pain, bruises, and hurts to Him. You are within His gentle yet strong arms. Open your heart and trust.

SECTION 1

BROKENNESS

CHAPTER 1

The Heart of Us

"Above all else, guard your heart, for everything you do flows from it" (Proverbs 4:23, NIV).

Sometimes when I am out and about absently wandering, my mind begins to drift. It drifts towards my day-to-day activities or the things that worry me. Sometimes my mind drifts towards my yesterday. Often my drifting leads to God and all He has done for me. All He has brought me through and the trials He is bringing me through now. During these times when I dwell on God, I can't help but notice people moving all around me. I focus on these people constantly moving, never taking a deep breath to slow everything down or seeing what is all around them. It is then I start to ponder: do they understand that everything they do has a ripple effect? Every decision that they make affects them or someone else in some form. Every place they walk, something happens, every person they talk to changes an outlook, and every choice they make causes a ripple in time, in history.

Every single person is connected, in unity with one another. Or at least that is how it's supposed to be, how God intended it to be. But something happened. From the very beginning, time and history were disrupted. Evil entered the world. An evil that has and can change the course of one person. This change can happen if that person so chooses to give over to that evil and hand over an important piece of themselves, their heart. This evil has caused God to give us a warning: "Above all else, guard your heart, for everything you do flows from it" (Proverbs 4:23, NIV).

Within this verse, three components need to be heeded. Let's start with the first component: guard. This means to stay alert, to protect, to be aware. You must guard your heart with a watchfulness, an astuteness. Today we can associate the word guard with a police officer. They guard those who are in danger and protect people who cannot defend themselves. When a police officer is in a position to guard, the officer will assess the situation, gather evidence, and make a calculated decision on how to guard someone in the most efficient way. This is also the same way you need to guard your heart. Essentially, besides God, you are the protector of your heart. You know the course of your heart; you know the hurts, the scars, and the joys of your heart. No one can guard your heart better than you can.

Just like a police officer, you have the power to guard your heart. God has given you that power through His truths. His truths are His Word. Within His Word is the truth of who your heart belongs to. You guard your heart with His love, His forgiveness, and His redemption. Reading, studying, and understanding the Word of God brings the revelation of His truths. God has given you His truths to enable you with His power to guard your heart. Understanding the truths that God has given you the power to use is critical. King Solomon understood this when he wrote, "Discretion will protect you, and understanding will guard you" (Proverbs 2:11, NIV). If you do not understand the kind of power that God's truths have on your heart, then your heart will become a desolated wasteland. It will be taken captive by the enemy, and your source of life will wither away.

Back to our police officer analogy, when a police officer guards someone, usually they are guarding because an enemy poses a threat to that person. Think of it like this: for every guard, there is an enemy. If there was no enemy, there would be no use for a guard. Your need to guard your heart is imminent. Your enemy is constantly after your heart. Not knowing the truths of who you are in God opens your heart to brokenness. As Peter warns us, "Be alert and of sober mind. Your enemy the devil prowls around like a roaring lion looking for someone to devour" (1 Peter 5:8, NIV). Rooting the truths of God in your heart will guard you against the enemy.

In college, I was an athlete, a basketball player. I went to a small private college, now a university. It's so small that to get from the dorms to classes was only about a seven-minute walk. Though the college itself was small, the athletics were on a different level. At least, much different than high school. The level of competitiveness was much greater. College ball was faster, bigger, and more intense. Throughout my high school career, I was the star on my team; I was the best player. So, I had all the confidence in the world coming into college. In all honesty, I was arrogant. However, in my first real college practice, I had my world shattered. My confidence shattered. I learned that everybody on the team was just as good as I or even better. There was no separation between the good and the bad. This shook me as a player but more as a person.

That first year in college, I struggled to incorporate myself into the team as a player. I was constantly competing for playing time, and I noticed that my weaknesses as a player were being exposed. I was not the fastest player nor the most athletic. Actually, I was one of the slowest on the team. I had to work twice as hard to make up for it.

For a player, this was devasting, and I thought things couldn't get any worse. Boy, was I wrong. I didn't make the varsity rotation. I was put on the JV team, but I was allowed to dress for the varsity games. That is when I truly crumbled. It was a crushing blow. I lost my confidence. And because I lost my confidence, I didn't see myself as worthy enough to play on the varsity level or worthy enough to use the gifts that God had blessed me with. Emotionally I was out of control, and I cared too much about what others thought of me. The root of my problem was exposed.

I had become so absorbed in basketball that I identified myself only as a basketball player. I forgot who I belonged to. I forgot my truths. My heart became broken by the false confidence, the unworthiness, the emotional turmoil, and the pleasing of others. My heart had become more cracked than it already was. What was most crushing is that I forgot who my God is. I forgot the goodness of Himself, all the sacrifices He made for me, and I forgot that He chose me first above all others. I had allowed the enemy to take precedent in my life and let him define who I was. My identity crisis was my lack of knowing God's truths, which resulted in my broken heart.

This leads me to my second component: the heart. I have been talking about guarding your heart with no explanation of what the heart is. Our heart is important to who we are as living beings. The Hebrew word for heart is *leb*. The Strong's Concordance defines *leb* as "heart, mind, midst."[1] Our heart is our inner man. It is the center of who we are in this life. Our emotions flow from the heart (Matthew 15:8), our desires come from the heart (Psalm 37:4), and our personality (thinking, wisdom, and will) is the heart (Philippians 4:8). Our heart is in the midst of us.

You see, the heart is what makes each one of us unique in this world filled with billions of people. From the beginning, God designed the heart to be good, but our hearts became infiltrated by the first sin. Until we come back to God and profess that Jesus is our Savior, accepting Him into our hearts, we will be filled with darkness instead of light. God gives us free will, and in giving us free will, we must choose a course of action. Our course of action can be of good, or it can be of evil. When we come to the cross-road of our choosing, God will test our hearts to determine the outcome. But the Word of God warns us, "The heart is deceitful above all things and beyond cure. Who can understand it?" (Jeremiah 17:9, NIV).

He must test the heart to see if we are faithful in our actions to Him. In Jeremiah 17:10 (NIV), God tells Jeremiah, "I the LORD search the heart and examine the mind, to reward each person according to their conduct, according to what their deeds deserve." Our hearts represent our true character, as we find this out in 1 Samuel 16. God sent Samuel to find the next king of Israel, which was David. When Samuel arrived at David's house, he met David's brothers. Samuel assumed God would choose one of his brothers, but Samuel was only looking at the outward appearance. Thus, when Samuel thought one of David's brothers was the right choice, God intervened and said to Samuel, "Do not consider his appearance or his height, for I have rejected him. The LORD does not look at the things people look at. People look at the outward appearance, but the LORD looks at the heart" (1 Samuel 16:7, NIV).

People look at the outside appearance because their eyes are blinded by what they want to see. God sees the true character, the true heart, because He is our heart. He is the designer, the Creator of our hearts. Nothing can be hidden from God.

Our heart is essential to God. This is why we must be careful in all aspects of the heart. King Solomon emphasizes this when he says, "As water reflects the face, so one's life reflects the heart" (Proverbs 27:19, NIV). As we choose the course of our hearts, we must be aware that one path leads to redemption, and the other path leads to more brokenness. God wants us to choose the path to redemption, but sometimes that isn't our first step. I learned this the hard way, when I allowed my emotions to hinder me and when my heart was more set on pleasing others than God. The result was I became someone I was not. I became a shell of myself: tentative, hesitant, worthless, angry, bitter, and broken. I was holding back the gifts that God blessed me with, and in turn, I rendered myself useless. I had lost my meaning. I had lost my purpose in this life.

When your heart is full of brokenness, how can you live your life to the fullness of who He created you to be? The answer is you can't. Everything that we do has a purpose, a purpose that affects our lives and the lives around us. It is God's will that we fulfill His purposes. But when you lose your purpose in this life that God has designed specifically for you, then you also lose your meaning in life. A heart full of brokenness is a heart empty of life. A life that God intends for you to be overfilled with. A life filled with meaning to pursue and accomplish His purposes to glorify Him with all your heart.

The last component of Proverbs 4:23 is life. God is the living God. He is the Giver of life. He alone can give or take life. Life depends upon God to keep everything in order. When Paul was speaking to the Athenians in Acts, he said,

The God who made the world and everything in it is the Lord of heaven and earth and does not live in temples built by human hands. And he is not served by human hands, as if he needed anything. Rather, he himself gives everyone life and breath and everything else.

Acts 17:24–25 (NIV)

He is the Creator of all things, and life is what only God can give (Deuteronomy 32:39), what He can only sustain (Psalm 119:116). God is the one who breathed life into man and woman. We became His image.

We became a part of Him, an extension of life. We must not take for granted this life He has gifted us with. The moment we take for granted this life is the moment that we are sent back to dust. It is the moment that we are separated from Him. In the Book of Job, Elihu was talking to Job and said, "If it were his intention and he withdrew his spirit and breath, all humanity would perish together and mankind would return to the dust" (Job 34:14–15, NIV). We must choose the Giver of life. We must choose to give our hearts to God. Let Him search and examine your heart (Psalm 139:23).

He gives life and takes life, but He blesses and curses. Our choices determine the blessings and the cursings we will receive. We can choose life choices, or we can choose death choices. I'm not talking about being alive with breath in your lungs or being dead in the grave. I'm talking about spiritual fruitful life choices and spiritual death choices. Spiritual life is dwelling in God; it is having His spirit within you and choosing to follow His ways above all other ways. Spiritual death is denying God, choosing to follow your own will and the ways of the world. The choice is up to you, but God calls us to choose life.

This day I call the heavens and the earth as witnesses against you that I have set before you life and death, blessings and curses. Now choose life, so that you and your children may live and that you may love the LORD your God, listen to his voice, and hold fast to him. For the LORD is your life, and he will give you many years in the land he swore to give to your fathers, Abraham, Isaac and Jacob.

Deuteronomy 30:19–20 (NIV)

It is paramount that we choose life in everything that we do because when trials hit and our hearts become involved, then the choice becomes confusing. Putting forth the effort to choose life in everything will prepare us for the broken heart.

We will not succumb completely to the pain, anger, hurt, and bitterness of a broken heart. Though choosing life and choosing death will become blurred, we have to remember that God has given this life as a gift. In doing so, we are an image of Him. He has put His living breath within us, squashing the breath of death that rises. The broken heart yearns for the fullness of life. It yearns to be alive in God. In John, Jesus says, "I have come that they may have life, and have it to the full" (John 10:10, NIV). Dear child, your heart was never supposed to be broken; it is never supposed to choose death. Your heart is meant to soar, it is meant to be full of life, and it is meant to be filled with the wholeness of God.

Chapter 2

Broken by Others

*"The Lord your God is with you, the Mighty Warrior who saves.
He will take great delight in you; in his love he will no longer
rebuke you, but will rejoice over you with singing"
(Zephaniah 3:17, NIV).*

When I was about sixteen, I went through one of the hardest trials in my life. At that time, I was not yet with God. I was on the edge. The edge of wanting to choose God but then taking a step back at the last second. I was on the edge of choosing spiritual life or choosing spiritual death. But this inferno trial I went through changed me greatly. It changed me mentally and emotionally. It left me with a broken heart and plenty of scars, but it also brought me to my God. It brought me to Jehovah Rapha (The Lord my Healer), the love of God, the forgiveness of Jesus, and the redemptive God.

At that time, I was living with my father back in my hometown. We had just moved from Washington State so that I could be on an AAU team to help further my basketball career. AAU stands for Amateur Athletic Union, and it is an organization that helps young girls and boys further their dream of becoming college athletes. Going back to the story, my mom and my siblings stayed behind so that they wouldn't have to be uprooted again. Before my father and I decided to move to my hometown, there was already dissension within the family. My parents got into fights often, and

I quarreled with my father. The situation within my family was turning negative quickly. Nonetheless, I went with my father, and for about two years, we lived together in my hometown.

The beginning of those two years was the start of my trial. It was the start of my fire that I had to go through. A little back story before I go further, my father was incredibly involved in my basketball. Anything basketball-related, we did together. It was during those times that my father and I created a strong bond with one another. In my eyes, he was my star. He was my hero. However, in those two years, our relationship became strained. It became so strained that eventually, our close bond with one another snapped in half, never able to fuse back together like it once was.

This was the beginning of my broken heart. In all that I did, he would push me to my limits. Sometimes beyond my limits. It's okay to be pushed to your limits, which helps you grow as an individual. It's not okay for those limits to be pushed where you become engrossed in the darkness. When he would push me beyond my limits, I would get frustrated and angry with him. This led to us bickering back and forth. Eventually, over time, that bickering turned into anger, and that anger spewed hurtful words. Those hurtful words became a snowball effect within our relationship.

Before I go any further, I want to make clear that nobody is perfect and that we all have some kind of problem within our lives. The same goes for my father. Like most problems, they had a negative impact on the people around him. His problem was he tended to get angry quickly, sometimes violently, and he became controlling, especially to the ones close to him. This anger and control, I experienced first-hand. There are multiple instances where I can describe my experiences, but I will only tell a few throughout this book. Right now, I will start with one. Understand that my broken heart was not broken all in one day or one week. My heart was gradually broken throughout my childhood. And in the span of two years, it became the focal point.

As I am writing this, I reflect on my life and see the first glimpse of who my father was at the age of twelve. I was diagnosed with Guillain-Barré syndrome (GBS). Guillain-Barré syndrome is "a rare disorder in which your body's immune system attacks your nerves."[2] GBS causes the whole body to become paralyzed. The rarity of this disorder is that for every 100,000 people, one person is affected.[3] Here is my experience with GBS.

On a warm summer day, I was playing baseball. I was at the plate waiting for the pitcher to throw the ball. I heard the crowd cheering while my heart was beating fast. The pitcher threw the ball. I tracked it with my eyes and hit it, sending the ball to the third baseman. I was stunned for a second and stood still. Then my father shouted, "Run, Kaela, run!" I ran as fast as I could but recognized something was off. My legs were not moving fast. Instead of a run, it was like I was jogging in slow motion. My breathing became heavily labored. I realized at that moment that something was very wrong with me. I couldn't run. Physically, I was not able to. After my realization, I don't remember what happened in the game, but I do remember what happened afterward.

My father questioned me why I didn't run fast, and I told him something was wrong. He proceeded to get angry with me and shouted at me to run to his car in the parking lot. To this day, I don't know why he got angry with me, but it led to a shouting match between us. I kept yelling at him that I couldn't run. The next thing he did was grab my left arm, and as we were walking down a hill, he took off at a dead sprint, dragging me with him. I tried to keep up, but my knees ended up getting scraped, and my arm was hurting from being stretched too much. He shoved me in his truck, and we drove home.

He was still terribly angry with me, and at this point, I was a sobbing mess. Once we got home, he gave me some chores to do. One of those chores was carrying thick, huge textbooks up the stairs into a room. I had four stacked up in my arms but struggled to carry them. I had struggled so much up the stairs that to support myself, I leaned a shoulder against the wall and used the wall to propel me upwards. For the next stack of textbooks that I had to carry, I tried to muster up as much strength as possible but couldn't make it up the stairs. When my father saw this, he got angrier and picked me up, placing me in my room.

The next thing I remember is my mom came home from work, sensing something was wrong with me. She put me through a couple of basic tests, but I failed to complete them. She immediately took me to the hospital, where I was diagnosed with GBS. I went through surgery, and as I came out of my drowsiness, I heard my parents arguing. My father was arguing with my mom that there was nothing wrong with me, that I was absolutely okay. Still to this day, he believes nothing is wrong with me. By the mercy of God, I did recover after spending about two weeks in the hospital. But the damage to my heart was already done. These events opened my eyes and splintered my heart.

Events like this kept stacking up, one after another, creating an atomic bomb, an atomic bomb that would eventually explode. Events like these made me question who I am, made me question the love of my father, and made me question my worthiness.

Before I continue with my story, I want to focus on the scripture at the beginning of the chapter. I want us to focus on the greatness and goodness of God. It's important that during our brokenness from others, we need to remember God is an Almighty God. He is ever there; He is our protector, our refuge, and our shelter. We need to remember that He is always for us and never against us. This might be hard to comprehend, but God does allow bad things to happen. He allows bad people to hurt His children. God is an all-knowing God. Though sometimes we cannot see His goodness during our trials, it is there bringing us through. He always turns the bad into good.

The chapter scripture is from Zephaniah 3:17 (NIV), "The Lord your God is with you, the Mighty Warrior who saves. He will take delight in you; in his love he will no longer rebuke you, but will rejoice over you with singing." Our focus will be on God as the warrior, God as the savior, the joyfulness of God, and the love of God.

God is more than a proven warrior; He is the first warrior, not just "a" warrior. There is only one true warrior, and that is Him. As His children, we are a part of His army and can be named a warrior, but we are not the first warrior, the true warrior. We need help fighting our battles and the war. We need a general, a warrior, to guide and fight alongside us. After the Israelites crossed the Red Sea, Moses sang a song to the Lord, and within the lyrics was this, "The Lord is a warrior; the Lord is his name" (Exodus 15:3, NIV). Being the warrior is who God is, and His warrior side is what we need during our brokenness.

The enemies of our brokenness may come at us with a sword and a spear, or they may come at us with hurtful words and actions that make us fear another, but we come against our enemies with the Warrior God. When David was on the battlefield getting ready to fight Goliath, he said, "You come against me with sword and spear and javelin, but I come against you in the name of the

Lord Almighty, the God of the armies of Israel, whom you have defied" (1 Samuel 17:45, NIV). David trusted and had faith in God to fight his battles. For the battles belong to the Lord. If we attempt to right the wrongs that were done to us, we will only become more heartbroken. It is not by our strength the enemy is defeated, but it is by the powerfulness of God.

When we become broken, it becomes difficult for us to fight our battles. To fight against who we were broken from. But our battles are not our own to fight. They are meant to be fought alongside God. The battles of our brokenness belong to Him. We have to look past our hurts and understand that God is our defender. We cannot fight alongside God with our brokenness blinding us. Each time we choose to see through our brokenness, we risk pulling further away from God. We risk choosing spiritual death and not the life God has gifted us with. Inevitably, others will hurt us. We live in a fallen world, but with the wisdom of God, we know that when the battle is given to Him, we will overcome our brokenness.

As a warrior, God saves His people. There are many ways He saves us through, such as deliverance, healing, provision, and many more. Our saving comes solely from God. No one and nothing else can save us. A person cannot save you from your brokenness. They can pray for you, or God can use them for His purpose, but ultimately, they are not the sole reason you are saved. You see, there is no substitute for the Savior. There is only one Savior, and that is God. "The Lord is my rock, my fortress and my deliverer; my God is my rock, in whom I take refuge, my shield and the horn of my salvation. He is my stronghold, my refuge and my savior—from violent people you save me" (2 Samuel 22:2–3, NIV).

You might be thinking, "What about Jesus?" Now, hold on, I haven't forgotten about Jesus; I mentioned Him already. I mentioned Him when I said God is solely our Savior. Jesus is God. Paul spoke of this in the Book of Romans when he said, "If you declare with your mouth, 'Jesus is Lord,' and believe in your heart that God raised him from the dead, you will be saved" (Romans 10:9, NIV).

Jesus is the ultimate model of brokenness. Unlike us, Jesus is sinless, He is holy, and He is purity. He came to change the world, to bring salvation to the lost, to bring forgiveness to all, and bring eternal life in God. However, in His era, people did not see Him as such. They saw Him as an enemy to their worldly principles.

> He had no beauty or majesty to attract us to him, nothing in his appearance that we should desire him. He was despised and rejected by mankind, a man of suffering, and familiar with pain. Like one from whom people hide their faces he was despised, and we held him in low esteem.
>
> Isaiah 53:2–3 (NIV)

These people decided to break Jesus. They didn't like the light that shined forth, exposing their darkness. They didn't like His honesty of who God is. That dislike turned into a hatred only the enemy could convey. We see this in the vivid descriptions of Isaiah,

> Surely he took up our pain and bore our suffering, yet we considered him punished by God, stricken by him, and afflicted. But he was pierced for our transgressions, he was crushed for our iniquities; the punishment that brought us peace was on him, and by his wounds we are healed. We all, like sheep, have gone astray, each of us has turned to our own way; and the LORD has laid on him the iniquity of us all. He was oppressed and afflicted, yet he did not open his mouth; he was led like a lamb to the slaughter,

and as a sheep before its shearers is silent, so he did not open his mouth. By oppression and judgment he was taken away. Yet who of his generation protested? For he was cut off from the land of the living; for the transgression of my people he was punished. He was assigned a grave with the wicked, and with the rich in his death, though he had done no violence, nor was any deceit in his mouth.

Isaiah 53:4–9 (NIV)

You are not the only one to experience brokenness by others. Jesus experienced it for you so you can relate with Him. His experience of brokenness brings the brokenhearted closer to Him. He understands your pains, hurts, and emotional turmoil because He went through the same things you did. He understands and knows your broken heart. The psalmist says, "The LORD is close to the brokenhearted and saves those who are crushed in spirit" (Psalm 34:18, NIV). Give Him your delicate heart because He is your Savior.

The miracle of Jesus is that He rose from the grave three days later. He may have been broken by others, but His heart was not crushed. You, too, can rise from your grave. You can rise from the brokenness of others. Turn to Jesus, who saves.

As you turn to Him, a joy will overtake you. This joy is the joyfulness of the Lord. A joyfulness that cannot be broken by the onslaught of others. Even through your own broken heart, joy is found. Joy is the fruitfulness of a right relationship with God. It is a delight in the Lord, and it is Him who takes delight in you.

In your broken heart, you are hurt, pained, angry, and bitter, but when you start to worship God, entering His presence, all that washes away. Worshiping Him ushers in the joyfulness of the Lord. It will not erase all the hurt, pain, anger, and bitterness, but it will focus your eyes on the one who will never forsake you nor leave you. His presence, the Holy Spirit, is "love, joy, peace, forbearance, kindness, goodness, faithfulness, gentleness and self-control" (Galatians 5:22–23, NIV). He will never hurt you; only bring joy.

Your focus will be turned to the joyfulness of your situation. When you take joy in your situation, it becomes bearable, it becomes less hurtful, and it becomes a balm to your heart. Joy is understanding that though your heart is broken, you will still give God the praise and the glory in your valley. The disciple James said, "Consider it pure joy, my brothers and sisters, whenever you face trials of many kinds, because you know that the testing of your faith produces perseverance" (James 1:2–3, NIV). James didn't just say happiness or joy; he said pure joy. Usher in pure joy during your situations.

Jesus is an example of ushering in pure joy when His heart was broken. Jesus knew that He would be crucified on the cross, that He would be tortured and mocked, but He still chose pure joy. He chose pure joy because of what He had to look forward to. He looked forward to sitting on the throne with His Father. We also have this same reward to look forward to with pure joy. For Jesus said, "So with you: Now is your time of grief, but I will see you again and you will rejoice, and no one will take away your joy" (John 16:22, NIV). Did you read that? Jesus said, "No one will take away your joy." It is completely yours to grab hold of and never let go! You were broken by others, and you feel as though pieces of you are missing, but your joy is not one of them. Your joy in God will fill those missing pieces, and you will have the pure joy of sitting at God's right hand and the joyfulness of being in His holy presence.

It's important to know that when joyfulness comes into your heart, the love of God also comes. God's love is not the love of this world. It is of you, His children. His love is for your aching heart. It is a soothing healing. God's love is unconditional love, a Father's love, and a fruitful love. The most descriptive love of God is found in Corinthians.

> Love is patient, love is kind. It does not envy, it does not boast, it is not proud. It does not dishonor others, it is not self-seeking, it is not easily angered, it keeps no record of wrongs. Love does not delight in evil but rejoices with the truth. It always protects, always trusts, always hopes, always perseveres. Love never fails.

> 1 Corinthians 13:4–8 (NIV)

This kind of love heals, forgives, transforms, and redeems us.

Everything our Father allows *for* us or allows to happen *to* us is out of love. Even allowing our hearts to be broken is out of love. Though we cannot understand His ways, we must know they are always for our good and out of love. God allowed His Son to be sacrificed for us. For love. He loved us so much that He let His Son be beaten, bruised, tortured, whipped, and crucified for our sins. In 1 John 4:10 (NIV), we see this: "This is love: not that we loved God, but that he loved us and sent his Son as an atoning sacrifice for our sins." Always God is for your greater good; He is always for you.

You must let His love heal your heart and fill up the cracks. If you do not allow it to happen, your relationship with God will be strained, and you will not see fruitfulness in your life. When you release the anger and bitterness, your heart will feel light as a feather. Your heart will seek the truth. It will start to seek what

God has been giving you from the start: love. Your heart and soul will love God with every fiber of your being. As love enters your heart, the fullness of God enters.

Zephaniah 3:17 resonates with my story because it shows me that God was constantly with me through my trials even though I could not see it. He was and is my warrior. His delight in me is my joy of Him, and His love for me brings me closer to Him. My brokenness is not my end; it's my beginning in Him. Fast forward to when I was sixteen and living with my father, the first couple of months were smooth sailing, but then we started to get into small arguments. Those small arguments turned into bigger arguments, and those bigger arguments turned into an abusive relationship. This abusive relationship was mentally and emotionally abusive.

In the house that we lived in, there was a wood-burning stove. A wood-burning stove is an iron stove that you burn wood in to keep the entire house warm. Around the stove could get messy. There would be wood chips and ash everywhere from opening and closing the stove. You would constantly need to clean out the ash. This was my routine chore every winter. But this routine chore became more than that.

One day, my father had asked me to sweep up the wood chips and clean out the stove. I grumbled a bit about not wanting to do it, but ultimately, I started to do as he asked. As I started to sweep the wood chips, he looked at me and said I was sweeping it up wrong. I asked him to tell me how he wanted it done, and he did. So, I started to sweep up the wood chips his way, but again he said I wasn't doing it right. At this point, he was starting to get angry with me. Instead of asking him to show me what to do, I kept on sweeping, ignoring him. This made him angrier, and before I knew it, he started screaming at me. The words I kept hearing over and over were that I was an idiot and that I couldn't do anything right. Over and over, I heard these words. By then, they were already imprinted into my heart.

Still, I ignored him, trying to keep my own emotions in check. I need you to understand that my father is the kind of person that if you show any signs of weakness or fear, he'll pounce on you. He will exploit your weaknesses and fear of him. As I was trying to finish my chore as quickly as possible, he grabbed me by the arm and shoved me. With his other hand, he grabbed my head on the side and pushed it up against the wall. As my head was smashed against the wall, he was screaming in my ear. It was more of a roar. He was roaring in my ear. This all happened in a flash, and I had no time to react to it. But the only emotion and feeling that coursed through my body was fear. This fear caused one thought to run through my mind: *He's going to hit me. I'm not strong enough to fend him off, and nobody is here to defend me. I am alone.* However, all of a sudden, he released me and stormed outside, roaring to the sky. I scrambled away and ran up to my room, locking my door. For hours, I didn't come downstairs for fear of him turning on me and hitting me.

I told you this story so that you can understand how God was there even when I couldn't see Him. Let me explain. Constantly being in fear of my father and absorbing his hurtful words into my heart was harmful to me, but my God was there. He was there when he stopped my father's anger from boiling over. He was there when He stopped my father from hitting me. He was there. I just couldn't see it at the time. Instead, what I saw was a father who became angry over a pile of wood chips because it wasn't cleaned up his way. What I felt was being scared and fearful. What I did was equate his hurtful words to who I was. What I saw, what I felt, and what I did led to the beginning of a broken heart. It was the beginning of a broken heart because, in all of that, I couldn't see my God working through it. I couldn't comprehend why He would allow the bad. Yet, I can't look at my lack of comprehension. I need to look and understand that He is my warrior who saved me from evil because He loves me.

He loves you. You are in the palm of His hands.

In John 16, Jesus is explaining to the disciples that He will be leaving soon but to be joyful in His departing because He will be coming back. So, in John 16:33 (NIV), at the end of His explanation, Jesus says, "I have told you these things, so that in me you may have peace. In this world you will have trouble. But take heart! I have overcome the world." Jesus knew the disciples would grieve because of the brokenness that He suffered for us. But Jesus reminded and encouraged them that He will be coming back. He rules over all things, including the brokenness of His people.

In this scripture, Jesus tells His disciples to focus on peace and that He has overcome the world. He also informs us that, in this world, we will have troubles (trials, tribulations, and brokenness). We need to expect the troubles of this world but expect with peace in our hearts and an understanding He has overcome the world leading to our sure victory. Without that expectation, our hearts are susceptible to being broken, and the victory will be far from our reach. However, Jesus understood that we will not always have peace, and we will forget that He overcame the world because we are human. He knew we would become broken by others. John 16:33 is our reminder of what we need to have in our hearts so we come out as victors.

Let's talk about peace and overcome. Merriam Webster's Dictionary defines peace in two different ways: 1) "a state without war" and 2) "freedom from disquieting or oppressive thoughts or emotions."[4] During our brokenness, we are in a war. This war isn't person versus person; this war is within us. It's a war between the pained you and the one who God created you to be. The pained you feels all the emotions of brokenness, and those emotions (of anger, bitterness, worry, fear, defeat) block out all that is of God. There is a wall that is erected within your heart that prevents the peace of God, the healing of God, and the love of God to overcome your brokenness. In John 16:33, Jesus' commandment was to have peace in Him, but this can't be accomplished if you are at war with yourself and your emotions are controlling you. Jesus sacrificed Himself so that He could bring everlasting peace into your life. "And the peace of God, which transcends all understanding, will guard your hearts and your minds in Christ Jesus" (Philippians 4:7, NIV). Remember, Jesus also went through brokenness, but He had peace because ultimately, God is the victor over brokenness. Let the peace of Jesus rule in your heart and your life because as one with Him, you were called to live in peace (Colossians 3:15). He did not call you to live in your brokenness. He called you to live in peace in Him.

Jesus knew that, in this world, troubles would abound. He didn't say troubles would possibly come or not come. He said troubles will come. No matter what season you are in, at some point, you will encounter troubles (trials). Therefore, Jesus commands us to take heart, meaning to be confident in Him because He has overcome the world. We see this in Revelation when the enemy rears its ugly head during the end times, bringing chaos and destruction. "They will wage war against the Lamb, but the Lamb will triumph over them because he is Lord of lords and King of kings—and with him will be his called, chosen and faithful followers" (Revelation

17:14, NIV). Even during the most perilous times, Jesus is the victory. He is the overcomer. If He has already overcome the end times and the enemy, don't you think He has already overcome your brokenness?

As believers of Jesus, we need to plant in our hearts that He has overcome our brokenness, that the enemy or other people will not break us because of our faith in Jesus. Yes, it takes faith to activate the power of Jesus to overcome in our lives. If we do not believe that Jesus is within us, within our hearts healing, forgiving, and redeeming, then our hearts will remain broken. We will remain angry, bitter, hateful, and saddened. "For everyone born of God overcomes the world. This is the victory that has overcome the world, even our faith. Who is it that overcomes the world? Only the one who believes that Jesus is the Son of God" (1 John 5:4–5, NIV). We must root this truth in our hearts. This is the truth of belief in the one who died for you and rescued you while you were yet still sinful. Jesus' shoulders are broad enough. Give Him your brokenness and let Him reign as King in your heart.

Looking back on my story, I never had peace within my heart, and I did not take to heart that Jesus overcame the world. Remember, I was not walking with Jesus yet. And because of that, my heart became more broken, more broken from the fact that I didn't know I had a Father who loved me so much He gave His only Son to be sacrificed. I became more broken because I didn't have peace knowing my Creator was the victor of my heart and the victor of my trials. But as I mentioned earlier, when I reflect on my trial, I see where God was. He was protecting me and shielding me from more brokenness. Not only was He doing that, but He was bringing me to Him. He was entering into my heart, and I didn't even know it.

CHAPTER 3

A Broken World

"The one who does what is sinful is of the devil, because the devil has been sinning from the beginning. The reason the Son of God appeared was to destroy the devil's work" (1 John 3:8, NIV).

From the beginning, we see the first instance of brokenness in the Bible. It all started with Adam and Eve, our ancestors. Let's start in Genesis. God created mankind as an image of Him. We were supposed to be all of His goodness, love, and wholeness. He created Adam first, from the dust of the ground, and breathed His life into Adam. Then God created Eve from Adam's rib, and she became Adam's "bone of my bones and flesh of my flesh" (Genesis 2:23, NIV). Both were naked before each other; they felt no shame and became as one. During this period of no shame was no brokenness; there was harmony within the world. There was an undeniable love between Adam and Eve. But there was an undeniable wholesome bond between God and His creation.

Then came the serpent. The enemy. Satan. Within Adam and Eve's world, there was one tree that they couldn't eat from, and that was the tree of knowledge of good and evil. The serpent approached Eve and deceitfully convinced her to eat from the tree. The serpent said, "For God knows that when you eat from it your eyes will be opened, and you will be like God, knowing good and evil" (Genesis 3:5, NIV). Eve fell for the deception, convinced Adam, and both ate from the tree. As soon as they ate, both of their eyes became opened. This was the first sinful act of mankind, and it was catastrophic. God disciplined them both, and the consequences of their actions became severe.

Brokenness entered the world. Eve and Adam ate from the tree because they wanted to become more like God, and in doing so, their hearts became broken, a selfish act that broke the heart into a million pieces. God was no longer the whole of their heart. He was not the sole reason for why their heart beat. Both wanted more from the world than what God gave them. This is the reason why our hearts cannot be trusted. For "the heart is deceitful above all things and beyond cure" (Jeremiah 17:9, NIV). This one sinful act ushered in the brokenness of the world.

You see, from the very beginning, we are broken individuals, every single one of us. Until we give our hearts over to Jesus, we will remain broken. Jesus is truly a gift from God. Adam and Eve didn't have the gift of Jesus to atone for their sins. They had goats and rams as blood sacrifices that only temporarily covered their sins. It was a temporary band-aid for their brokenness, not truly healing and closing the cracks within the heart. Today, we have Jesus to completely wipe away our sins when we sincerely repent. He is our holy, pure, and clean sacrifice. He is the wholeness of our brokenness. He is not some temporary salve that goes away; He is the complete Healer with the cleansing of His blood.

Brokenness is the result of sin. This can be because of our sins or the sins of others that cause our brokenness. Either way, sin is the result of brokenness. We saw that with Adam and Eve; we saw that with Moses when He disobeyed God at the rock of Meribah, and we saw this with countless others. The sinfulness of the world has brought and caused much heartache to people. An extreme example of this is World War II, when Hitler committed genocide on millions of Jews. His main sin was murder, and because of what happened in that war, there was a ripple effect that changed the course of history. Countless people became broken, and not just the Jews but all the people that were affected by the war. The horrors of that war stayed with people day and night. People lost loved ones that could never be replaced, and the way we saw each other changed overnight.

Another example is modern-day slavery or human trafficking. Millions of girls, boys, women, and men are trafficked across the world for many reasons. The horrors they go through cannot even be imagined. The brokenness that takes hold of their hearts is dire. Many collapse and cave into the sin of this world. Their hearts become hardened to the point of irrevocable retrieval. The heart becomes bitter, angry, and depressed at the offenders and even at God.

When we sincerely turn our broken hearts to God, then true freedom is grasped. He is the only one who can make the heart whole. If your heart is chained by hurt, anger, offense, prejudices, or hate, then your freedom is far. You are still a broken individual. You must let go of all and surrender to the one who is pure.

> For God so loved the world that he gave his one and only Son, that whoever believes in him shall not perish but have eternal life. For God did not send his Son into the world to condemn the world, but to save the world through him. Whoever believes in him is not condemned, but whoever does not believe stands condemned already because they have not believed in the name of God's one and only Son. This is the verdict: Light has come into the

world, but people loved darkness instead of light because their deeds were evil.

John 3:16–19 (NIV)

During my journey, I chained my heart with bitterness, anger, pain, and hurt. Because of my chains, I did not let God be the whole of me. My chains were my comfort zone. Let me continue with my story.

My father and I constantly battled. These battles weren't with punches or kicks, but they were with words—hurtful, mean, angry words. These were words stuck within my heart, attempting to define who I was.

When I was with my father, I got into trouble a lot. Sometimes I would talk back, and sometimes I would cop an attitude. Mostly, I was a normal teenager, thinking my way was always right, and I was an adult who could make their own sound decisions. There were times when I got into trouble, and instead of explaining to me what I did wrong, my father would lose his temper. Once he lost his temper, things turned ugly quickly. I remember one day I was struggling to do my chores. He came into the room to inspect how I was doing, and I asked for help. Instead of helping me, he started calling me names. Even after I had finished with my chores, he continued to call me names. Weeks later, it continued. I had started to believe that I was those names. I believed those labels. I equated it to my worth. I know some may think it's just words, but to me, those words mattered.

Finally, fed up and with tears in my eyes, I yelled at him to stop calling me names. He dismissed my cry and continued. There were nights I cried all night long. I cried for it to stop. I cried because

I didn't know what I had done wrong. I cried because that was who I thought I was. I cried because I hated him.

Some of the most heart-breaking words he ever said to me were, "You are the worst daughter I ever had." When those words were said, my heart stopped beating for a second, and I allowed them to mold into my heart, taking that as the truth of who I am. For years I harbored that truth. I let his words define who I was. I saw myself as worthless.

It took me seven years to heal from all the hurtful words. It took me seven years to accept God's truth of who I am. It took my heart seven years to define that I am chosen by God, adopted by God, redeemed by God, forgiven by God, saved by God, loved by God, and God's masterpiece (Ephesians 1–2).

Bringing this full circle, my father was not walking with God; to this day, he still doesn't. Yet, he knows of God but chooses to reject Him. He lives a sinful life. Remember, Adam and Eve were the first to sin, which caused a catastrophic ripple across history forever. Everyone is born into sin until they choose to give their life to Jesus, accepting Him as their Savior. At the start of my father's life, he didn't choose to live in sin, but once he became cognizant of the workings of the world and God, a choice had to be made. Choose to accept God or reject God. He chose to reject God and consequently live a sinful life. Because he was not walking with God, this sin controlled his life. The enemy controlled his life.

To build upon this, I want us to look at 1 John 3:8 (NIV), "The one who does what is sinful is of the devil, because the devil has been sinning from the beginning. The reason the Son of God appeared was to destroy the devil's work." This scripture packs a punch that enlightens us on numerous things. Some things we have already dived into, and others, we dipped our toe. The first thing we dipped our toe in is those who willingly keep on sinning, the second is the enemy (the devil), and the third is the appearance of Jesus. In all three, we will find the reasons for our broken world.

Let's start by looking at the first reason, those who willingly keep on sinning. We see John also states that those who willingly keep on sinning are of the enemy. The enemy has control over them because they have relinquished that control. These people are choosing to reject God even when they know Him. In this world, many people know of God but reject Him increasing the possibility of brokenness to others. While it is important to note that people are openly rejecting God, we also need to take note of the sin aspect. As I said before, brokenness is the result of sin.

Sin is bondage (Proverbs 5:22), a slave driver (John 8:34), costly (Acts 7:60), deadly (Romans 5:12), and a killer (Romans 7:11). Sin stalks its prey and casts "a long, dark shadow over the rest of human history."[5] My earthly father stands in that dark shadow, and he chooses to stay within that shadow. Because sin is prevalent in his life, that sin is a leash around his neck. He has become a slave of the world. This world is heartbreaking, evil, and controlled by the enemy. Everything the enemy represents is sin. Sin is being against God, which parallels the enemy's goal that is to turn you away from God. To put you in chains. Our God is freedom, and the enemy is the bondage of sin. The brokenness of the world is a result of the sin in this world, a sin that originated from Adam and Eve. A sin that the enemy wants all of us to stay in the shadows of.

Understand that as a Christian who sincerely seeks the heart of God, you are a target of the enemy. You are number one on his hit list. He will come at you with vicious attacks, using methods of deceit, lies, accusations, and temptations. He comes for your heart while using people who walk in his ways. As Christians, we leave our hearts open for such attacks. We forget that we are not battling with the people who hurt us; rather, it is the enemy within the people we are at battle with. We are at battle with their sinful heart.

But we cannot give the excuse that the enemy is always the cause of people hurting others. Sometimes, people are just hurtful, hateful, spiteful, and angry without the enemy's influence. When we are attacked, our hearts become flayed open, and brokenness settles in. Bitterness, anger, hurt, and pain encompass us, and we decide to blame God or the people who hurt us. But the Scriptures reveal that we do not wrestle with "flesh and blood, but against the rulers, against the authorities, against the powers of this dark world and against the spiritual forces of evil in the heavenly realms" (Ephesians 6:12, NIV).

God is not to blame for our brokenness. Does He allow certain things to happen to us? Yes. Is it to harm us? No. God is always for us. Look at the story of Joseph. Joseph's father favored him more than any of his other sons, resulting in giving Joseph a robe. This decision only maximized the visceral hate that Joseph's brothers had for Joseph. To further those feelings of hate, at a young age, Joseph had two dreams. The first dream was of sheaves. Joseph's sheave rose, but the other sheaves, which were of his brothers, bowed down to Joseph's sheave. The second dream was of the sun, moon, and stars bowing down to him. Joseph told his brothers, and his brothers hated him more for it. Out of their hatred bred murder. As Joseph went to get his brothers from the field, they were plotting his murder. They attacked him and threw him down a well. Instead of leaving Joseph to die, they stripped him of his robe and sold him as a slave. His brothers killed a goat, dipped

Joseph's coat in it, and returned to their father, claiming Joseph was killed by an animal.

As a slave in Egypt, Joseph came to serve the captain of the guard, Potiphar. God was with Joseph throughout his servitude, and he prospered. Potiphar saw how God was with Joseph, so Potiphar entrusted Joseph with his entire household. Now, Potiphar's wife had her eyes on Joseph, and she wanted to sleep with him, but he did not want to betray Potiphar. However, Potiphar's wife was insistent, desperate, and she deceived Joseph. One day when he went into the house, there were no household servants, and she surprised him by grabbing onto his cloak, desperately clinging to him and saying she wanted to sleep with him. Immediately Joseph turned and ran, tearing his cloak in her hand. That same day, she deceived her husband, Potiphar, and claimed Joseph raped her. Potiphar believed her, and he threw Joseph into prison. Once again, Joseph was betrayed.

While in prison, there were two other people with Joseph: the cupbearer and the baker to the king. One of the gifts that God blessed Joseph with was interpreting dreams. Both the cupbearer and the baker each had a dream, and Joseph interpreted them. At the end of his interpretation of the cupbearer's dream, he asked him to remember him. The cupbearer was restored to serving the king, but he did not remember Joseph, and the baker was killed. By this point, two years had passed since the cupbearer was restored to his position in the king's court. One night Pharaoh had a dream, and he needed it interpreted. He called the magicians and the wise people of Egypt to interpret, but they could not. Finally, the cupbearer remembered Joseph and told Pharaoh that Joseph could interpret his dream. Pharaoh pulled Joseph out of prison, and Joseph interpreted his dream successfully. Everything came to pass in the dream, resulting in Pharaoh promoting Joseph to oversee the whole land of Egypt.

There was a great famine in Egypt, and people from all over came to Pharaoh seeking food that Joseph oversaw. Some of the people that came were Joseph's brothers. When they first came to Joseph, they did not recognize him. At first, Joseph tested them to see where their hearts lay. His brothers passed the test, and in the end, Joseph revealed himself. They were overcome with guilt and surprise. Joseph was joyful to see his brothers, the same ones that tried to murder him and sold him as a slave.

I told you this whole story because, at the end of Genesis 50:20 (NIV), Joseph told his brothers, "You intended to harm me, but God intended it for good to accomplish what is now being done, the saving of many lives." God did allow bad things to happen to Joseph, and I'm sure Joseph wanted to cave into his circumstances, blaming God. But he didn't. Joseph did not allow all the bad things to define him, causing brokenness within his heart. He could have. He could have when he was sold as a slave, he could have when he was falsely accused of rape, and he could have when he was in prison. Time after time, Joseph could have been broken by his circumstances, and he could have let his heart turn bitter, angry, and hateful towards the people of this world. The same goes for us. We can be bitter, angry, and hateful to the people who cause our brokenness, or we can look to the one who only intends for our good—the only one who is our rescuer.

Joseph stayed true to the truth. He did not allow the sins of others to determine his destiny. He trusted in God and had utter faith in Him that He is in control over all circumstances: the good and the bad. He understood that God's purposes are always for our good. God says to His people in Jeremiah 24:6 (NIV), "My eyes will watch over them for their good, and I will bring them back to this land. I will build them up and not tear them down; I will plant them and not uproot them."

The second reason for our broken world is the enemy or the devil. Our enemy has one distinct goal in mind: animosity toward God. Simply put, the enemy hates God and any aspect of God. That means the enemy hates you. He wants to turn you away from God and to serve him. He is the tempter and the accuser. He creates havoc and incites hatred against one another. Where God is, be assured that the devil is not far behind. The devil does not want God's children to know the truth and to prosper. He wants to keep God's children locked up in the dark shadows, let their hearts wither away, and deceive them, letting them think that God has forsaken them or will not rescue them. Oh yes, we must guard our hearts against the enemy. He is only here "to steal and kill and destroy" (John 10:10, NIV).

The enemy will use other people to accomplish his tasks of destroying Christians. As Christians, we sometimes can't recognize this. All we see is our broken heart and the person who caused the brokenness. We don't see the darker forces at work. We start to blame other people, and eventually, we start to blame God. This is what the enemy wants, to turn us away from God, to not take comfort and shelter in His arms. Peter warns us to "[b]e alert and of sober mind. Your enemy the devil prowls around like a roaring lion looking for someone to devour" (1 Peter 5:8, NIV). If we are not sober and alert, then surely, our hearts will become broken. We will become the prey in the lion's mouth.

When we face and recognize the enemy, we must be ready to go to battle. You cannot run away or hide because he will find you. He is out to annihilate you. He is coming for your precious heart. To combat this, the Scriptures tell us,

> Be strong in the Lord and in his mighty power. Put on the full armor of God, so that you can take your stand against the devil's schemes. For our struggle is not against flesh and blood, but against the rulers, against the authorities, against the powers of this dark world and against the spiritual forces of evil in the heavenly realms. Therefore put on the full armor of God, so that when the day of evil comes, you may be able to stand your ground, and after you have done everything, to stand. Stand firm then, with the belt of truth buckled around your waist, with the breastplate of righteousness in place, and with your feet fitted with the readiness that comes from the gospel of peace. In addition to all this, take up the shield of faith, with which you can extinguish all the flaming arrows of the evil one. Take the helmet of salvation and the sword of the Spirit, which is the word of God.

> Ephesians 6:10–17 (NIV)

Jesus was tested and tempted by the enemy in the wilderness. Jesus had just been baptized by John the Baptist, and the Holy Spirit fell upon Him. By the leading of the Holy Spirit, Jesus went into the wilderness, fasting for forty days and forty nights. During these long days and nights, Jesus was tempted by the devil. The devil tempted Jesus three times, and all three times, Jesus used the written Word of God, proclaiming who His identity lay in. After Jesus rebuked the devil for the third time, the devil left.

You may be thinking, "But this is Jesus we're talking about! He is God and mighty over all things! It is easy for Jesus to rebuke the enemy! There is no way He was ever tempted!" However, you are not taking in the fact that Jesus fasted for forty days and forty nights. Most of us can't even fast for a day before we are running to the fridge eating all that is in sight! Jesus was tempted, and He did want what the enemy was proclaiming. How could He not? The power to take whatever He wants is within Him. He is Lord. What God is Jesus is. So yes, Jesus was very much tempted. Because of this temptation, we can relate to Him more.

When we are broken, our biggest temptation is our emotions. The enemy tempts us towards bitterness, anger, hate, and sadness. All this will achieve is a more broken heart, and it turns us away from God. But when we look at Jesus' temptation, we are reminded that we can overcome it. We need to put on the full armor of God, using the Word of God to have victory over the enemy and our brokenness. You cannot follow in the footsteps of the world, where emotions run rampant. There, you will be utterly destroyed, and your heart will be ripped into a million pieces. Instead, hold fast to the promises of God and your identity in Him. I leave you with this encouraging scripture that will bring all-encompassing confidence in our God.

> Then war broke out in heaven. Michael and his angels fought against the dragon, and the dragon and his angels fought back. But he was not strong enough, and they lost their place in heaven. The great dragon was hurled down— that ancient serpent called the devil, or Satan, who leads the whole world astray. He was hurled to the earth, and his angels with him. Then I heard a loud voice in heaven say: "Now have come the salvation and the power and the kingdom of our God, and the authority of his Messiah."
>
> Revelation 12:7–10 (NIV)

Our last reason for a broken world is Jesus. I don't mean that Jesus is the cause for a broken world but that Jesus is the *answer* to our broken world. He has overcome our brokenness at the cross. The shedding of His blood is the shedding of our brokenness. When we submit fully, wholly, and vulnerably to Jesus, then our brokenness is no longer our bondage. "Because the one who is in you is greater than the one who is in the world" (1 John 4:4, NIV). That is why Jesus is called the Savior: because He saves us from our brokenness, destruction, and torment. As we call upon the name of Jesus, we are calling Him to bring an inward change. An inward transformation. We cannot be satisfied with our hearts cracked. We must push into Jesus for our hearts to be completely healed and transformed by the blood of the Lamb.

We cannot let the sins of this world dictate the shape of our hearts. For to do that would be detrimental to the transformation of our hearts. He came so that our hearts would be set free from the chains of brokenness. Once we realize how powerful the blood of Jesus is, no sin, no enemy, and no world can stop us from soaring on eagle's wings. We will feel the air on our faces and the sun warming our skin. We will feel the ice melt from our hearts, beating with the blood of Jesus. In the Book of Ephesians, Paul explains to the Ephesian believers that he prays for them and what he prays for. As you read these verses that I am about to share with you, put yourself in the Ephesian believers' shoes. Let Paul pray for you.

> I pray that the eyes of your heart may be enlightened in order that you may know the hope to which he has called you, the riches of his glorious inheritance in his holy people, and his incomparably great power for us who believe. That power is the same as the mighty strength he exerted when he raised Christ from the dead and seated him at his

right hand in the heavenly realms, far above all rule and authority, power and dominion, and every name that is invoked, not only in the present age but also in the one to come. And God placed all things under his feet and appointed him to be head over everything for the church, which is his body, the fullness of him who fills everything in every way.

Ephesians 1:18–23 (NIV)

SECTION 2
PROUD HEART

CHAPTER 4

Our Downfall

Remember how the LORD your God led you all the way in the
wilderness these forty years, to humble and test you in order to
know what was in your heart, whether or not you would keep
his commands. He humbled you, causing you to hunger and then
feeding you with manna, which neither you nor your ancestors
had known, to teach you that man does not live on bread alone
but on every word that comes from the mouth of the LORD
(Deuteronomy 8:2–3, NIV).

In the previous section, we talked about brokenness and the various ways we can become broken. The ways our hearts can become broken are by the brokenness of other people and the brokenness of the world. As we know, our brokenness can cause an array of emotions that can turn our hearts away from God. But one emotion and sin that I have not mentioned is pride. The question that circles the mind is: how can a broken person be prideful? Well, I'm glad you asked because this is an emotion and sin we need to squash. Killing our prideful hearts is critical to receiving our forgiveness, healing, and redemptive heart.

To answer that question, we turn towards two scriptures: Deuteronomy 8:2 and Deuteronomy 8:3. These verses are ones of exhortation. Deuteronomy 8 is an account where Moses was prompting the Israelites to remember the God who brought them out of Egypt (the bondage), who crushed the Pharaoh's army in the Red Sea, who never left them when they turned their backs on Him, and who has always been their provision. As Moses exhorts the Israelites, we also need to be exhorted in our God.

The first scripture I want to focus on is Deuteronomy 8:2. Breaking this verse down, we need to look at the words "remember," "wilderness," "humble," and "heart." Let's start with "remember," which is at the beginning of the verse. "Remember how the LORD your God led you all the way in the wilderness these forty years, to humble and test you in order to know what was in your heart, whether or not you would keep his commands." First things first, we need to understand that God is the same today, yesterday, and forever. He has never changed. Not in our past, not in our present, and not in our future. We need to remember that. Before our brokenness, He is the same; during our brokenness, He is the same, and after our brokenness, He is the same. It is us who change, whether for good or for bad. It is okay to change. God did not create us to remain the same as He. If we did, then we would not become broken, and we would not grow. We are not God. We are changing people. That is how He created us. But we do need to remember who our God is during our brokenness, for He is the only one who can forgive, heal, and redeem.

When we remember and experience how God has brought us through in the past, then we can have trust and faith for what He is going to do for us in the future. The writer of Psalm 77:11–12 (NIV) says, "I will remember the deeds of the LORD; yes, I will remember your miracles of long ago. I will consider all your works and meditate on all your mighty deeds." Not only do we remember God, but God will remind us of His awesome gifts and blessings He did for us. When we remember and are reminded of the things of God, then the journey of our brokenness becomes easier. It becomes easier because we can put in our hearts the goodness and lovingness of God. We understand that He will never leave us nor forsake us during times of trouble or times of victory. He established that for us for what He did in our past and for what He is going to do in the future.

In our remembrance is the power of God. A power that we can use on our behalf to overcome our brokenness. Yet, also in our remembrance is the fine edge of walking in pride. When God wants us to remember what He did for us, He needs us to use it as strength, wisdom, forgiveness, healing, and redemption for our brokenness. This is the power He supplies to us in our remembrance of Him. He does not want us to remember so we can puff up our chests and proclaim God's victories as our own. This would certainly be our ruin and downfall. But more, it would cause unspeakable, catastrophic heartbreak for us.

This leads to my next focus point: "wilderness." Deuteronomy 8:2 (NIV) says, "Remember how the LORD your God led you all the way in the wilderness these forty years…" Now, I am going to go back to the word "remembrance" for just a second. In Deuteronomy 8:2, Moses is telling the Israelites that God wants them to remember all the miraculous deeds and wonderful signs He did for them, such as splitting the Red Sea in half and crushing the Pharaoh's mighty army. More importantly, God wants them to remember how He led them out of the wilderness that they wandered for forty years because of strife, disobedience, and worshipping other gods. This wilderness is what I want to focus on, but more specifically, why the wilderness was even mentioned in this verse.

When we think of wilderness, we imagine various types of trees, luscious vegetation, sun shining through the leaves, and a bountiful of animals. We see it as a wonder, a fantasy world. But what the Israelites saw as the wilderness is traversing through a desert with no place to call home, fighting numerous enemies, and relying solely on God for provision and protection. Their wilderness was a hard walk. At times the wilderness was even deadly. For forty years, they roamed their wilderness because of disbelief, disobedience, worshipping of other gods, and rejection of God. During their roaming, an incessant number of complaints were voiced, sin was rampant, and the blaming of God for their circumstances was constant. At one point, the Israelites wanted to go back to Egypt to stop the wandering of their troubles. They wanted to go back to their bondage, back to being overworked, back to being debased as human beings, and back to being broken. Yet, even with all their complaints, worshipping other gods, sin, and rejection, God still provided for them, protected them, fought for them, and chose them as His people, even through it all.

The Israelites weren't supposed to wander the wilderness for forty years. They were meant to get from point A to point B. They were meant to receive their inheritance, which was promised so long ago to Abraham. Instead, they chose the forty-year course because of their lack of faith in God. This lacking of faith caused brokenness that almost overcame them and took them further away from Him.

We must see that in our brokenness, we are walking this same wilderness as the Israelites. We are so consumed with our circumstances and our emotions that we let our brokenness determine the course for us. Then, we get stuck on the course, and we think we see a way out, but it is only the door of pride. This pride during our wilderness has a steep price. Most of the time, when we are broken and trying to navigate our way through the wilderness, we tend not to ask for help. We become very prideful in this aspect. We let our brokenness define us. We start to only trust in ourselves because of the hurt we've received from other people or the world. A fortified wall is erected around our hearts, and we fight anyone who tries to take down those walls. A broken heart hates vulnerability and hates the risk of getting hurt. Thus, all intrusions are shot down immediately, including God, and pride enters the heart. Then, the wilderness becomes barren, dark, and painful.

When our broken, prideful hearts take the lead, God becomes a mere shadow in our eyes. This scripture from Isaiah best describes how God views our disregard for Him because of pride.

> When I came, why was there no one? When I called, why was there no one to answer? Was my arm too short to deliver you? Do I lack the strength to rescue you? By a mere rebuke I dry up the sea, I turn rivers into a desert; their fish rot for lack of water and die of thirst. I clothe the heavens with darkness and make sackcloth its covering.
>
> Isaiah 50:2–3 (NIV)

God does not give up. He finds ways after ways to open our hearts. He disrupts our prideful streak and destroys it after we choose Him above our circumstances, above our wilderness, and above our pride.

Let me tell you my story of walking through the wilderness. As I was going through my mental and emotional experiences with my father, I felt as if I was stranded. I felt that no one was there to pull and push me out. To be frank, I think my wilderness was not a desert like the Israelites'. My wilderness was an imaginary ocean. In my mind, I could see myself barely treading water. My head would go under then come back up. My arms were burning from constantly keeping my body up, and my legs were losing strength, no longer wanting to kick. I was drowning. I wanted to give up and let the ocean pull me under, never to resurface again. It was easier to give up. I didn't have to struggle anymore. The temptation was alluring, and a few times, I almost gave in, but something inside of me refused to let go. Something inside of me wanted to keep fighting. Something inside of me wanted to be a warrior.

As a warrior, I didn't want my father to win the war. I would not give him the satisfaction of winning by name-calling, anger, or hurtful words. The ever-increasing fear inside of me, I could not let him see. I didn't want to be controlled anymore. I didn't want him to control what I was, who I was with, and what I did. I didn't want to drown; I wanted to live. I kept fighting battle after battle, no matter how exhausted and how weak I was. This wilderness was full of ferocious waves and raging storms. I was not just in the fight for my life; I was in the fight for my soul. Coming out of the wilderness could not be done on my own. I would not come out unscathed either. I needed help. I needed divine intervention. I needed a God who was bigger than my circumstances, bigger than my hurts, and bigger than the enemy.

God was there during my wilderness, and He is here now. When I decided to fully surrender myself over to Him, the war was won. There were still battles to be had, but the overall war was won. With God, every war is already our victory. Let me tell you one experience in my wilderness. One night after my father had gone to sleep, I was startled awake. Then, an all-consuming fear shot through my body. I will never forget this kind of bone-chilling fear. My room was adjacent to my father's, so I could see the end of the bed and the window. When I scanned his room, my eyes landed directly on the bed. Normally, in the dark, I could see the outline and shape of what was in the room, but that night I could not even see my hand in front of me. More fear shot through me as I stared, then I turned my eyes to my closet door. I knew that something was in there just as I knew something very evil was inside my father's bedroom. I pulled my covers over half my face, and I remember feeling as if someone or something was staring at me, never taking their eyes off me like a stalker. Then as my eyes scanned my room again, I could see the darkness rushing towards me, consuming me. I just remember thinking *I don't want to die. I don't want to die.* All of a sudden, I remembered to speak the name of Jesus when evil was around. I spoke Jesus' name softly at first. The darkness kept coming. Then, I spoke His name more forcefully and loudly. Of a sudden, the darkness vanished, and the moon illuminated my whole room like it was daytime. As if that wasn't enough protection, God sent three angels to that house. One was protecting me inside my room, and the others were on the rooftop guarding.

You see, God is in our wilderness. When we feel all is lost and see the never-ending darkness surrounding us, our God is in the midst.

> In a desert land he found him, in a barren and howling waste. He shielded him and cared for him; he guarded him as the apple of his eye, like an eagle that stirs up its nest and hovers over its young, that spread its wings to catch them and carries them aloft. The LORD alone led him; no foreign god was with him.
>
> Deuteronomy 32:10–12 (NIV)

He is our eagle, our protector, and our shield. The wilderness cannot overcome us, but we overcome it by surrendering wholly and fully to God.

Our wilderness cannot become our comfort zone. Allowing this allows for our brokenness to be our comfort. We become stubborn about letting go, and that stubbornness can turn into pride. A pride that says, "Only you can come out of the wilderness, and only you can fix your brokenness." All too often, this pride enters many Christians during their wilderness walk. Because of this, they stay stuck in their wilderness, never healing, forgiving, and redeeming properly. Pride blinds the eyes, and our brokenness cracks the heart. This combination is deadly, and our enemy knows it.

This leads to my next point: "humility." Going back to our Israelite story, we know they wandered the wilderness for forty years, and some of the causes were disobedience, worshipping other gods, and sinful deeds. But one cause that I have mentioned numerous times is pride. The Israelites thought they didn't need God to rule over nations. They thought they were the ones to come out of the wilderness by themselves. However, as we know, God was the one who defeated the enemy nations, and He was the one who placed the Israelites in a position to be kings. In Deuteronomy 8:2 (NIV) when it says, "Remember how the LORD your God led you all the way in the wilderness these forty years, to humble and test you…" Moses wants the people to remember that they wandered the wilderness for forty years because of the prideful streak they had. And this walk through the wilderness was to humble them before God because He wanted their hearts to be right.

Now, let's talk about the word "humility." Humility is a godly character (Matthew 11:29). It is wisdom (Proverbs 11:29) and meekness (Zephaniah 3:12). Humility is being humble before God like a child (Matthew 18:2–5). Our humility is the fear of the Lord. Not a frightening, scared kind of fear, but a reverence kind of fear. A fear that doesn't hurt us, but a fear that is for us.

Reverence fear is only possible when we are humble before God, then clothed in His righteousness. If pride enters our hearts during the wilderness and our brokenness remains our comfort, then we are living a dead spiritual life. We are letting the enemy control our lives. We then become unrighteous, which prevents us from having a place in heaven, especially since our hearts are still broken, carrying anger, bitterness, hate, sadness, and pride.

I mentioned in Chapter 1 my love for basketball and the difficulties I had my freshman year. I want to share with you my experiences with pride and a broken heart, the deadly combination. Entering college basketball my freshman year, I had an impressive list of accomplishments. In high school, I scored over two thousand points and roughly averaged about twenty-five points per game. I was feeling good about myself coming in. In all honesty, I was arrogant. I came in thinking that I was going to be the star on the team without putting in the work and that I was going to see a lot of playing time. I thought that I already had a spot on the team and was going to be the "it" factor. I thought all of that. In reality, none of that happened. The complete opposite took effect.

Immediately, in my first practice, I was knocked off my high horse. I realized my teammates were either just as good as I or better. My confidence dipped low, my identity became scrambled, and all the emotional and mental baggage I carried rose to the top. All of this progressed through the whole season, and it was just building up inside of me day by day. A side note: I had developed negative coping mechanisms during the time I spent with my father. For example, when my father yelled or screamed at me, I would shut off all emotions so I wouldn't get hurt. I protected my heart around a sheet of metal.

The negative coping mechanisms I developed were used during this trying time. One of the coping mechanisms I developed was I wouldn't speak about what was happening to me or what was wrong. So, when I had bad practices, I never told anyone. I just kept it all locked up inside of me. I kept all the negative emotions locked up within. But thank goodness, my mom and grandma could read me like a book because they picked up on my unhappiness, my hurt, and my aching heart right away. Little by little, they peeled back my layers and uncovered the true root of the problem. Though I was unhappy, I was hurt, and my heart was cracked, the root of my problem was pride. It was pride and a broken heart from my experiences with my father. After being beaten down time after time, God revealed the pride and broken heart within me.

During my time with my father leading up to my freshman year of college, I was walking through the wilderness. But somewhere during that time, I developed a prideful and broken heart. I thought I was the one to accomplish all my basketball feats; thus, when I went into college, I thought I was the one who was going to see myself through to accomplish better and greater things than I did in high school. All I thought was of myself. Never did I equate into the equation, God. Never did I take into consideration that God was the one who accomplished everything. And never did I glorify God for those accomplishments. I glorified myself, and this glorification led to the development of pride.

On top of a prideful heart, I had a broken heart that I never let heal. This heart was cracked in so many places that super glue and duct tape couldn't fix it. My heart was starving for unconditional love; it was starving for an identity, it was starving for healing, it was starving for redemption, and it was starving for God. My heart was also wrought with an all-consuming fear of my earthly father. Yes, I was very much afraid of my father. Afraid of getting hurt, afraid of being controlled again, and afraid of what he was capable of.

My heart was broken.

Ultimately, being prideful and being broken led to my downfall. Because of the problems I caused and the brokenness I harbored, my downfall was like hitting a concrete wall over and over again, never making a dent. In Proverbs, it says, "When pride comes, then comes disgrace, but with humility comes wisdom" (Proverbs 11:2, NIV). I did bring disgrace upon my life. I acted a fool, and because of that foolishness, I didn't see any playing time my freshman year, and I didn't listen to anyone, least of all God. My heart was hardened like Pharaoh in the Book of Exodus.

Eventually, when I fell off my high horse, I started to remember, recognize, hear, and see what was happening. I looked towards God to humble me and to heal me. The journey to climb back up the mountain and out of my wilderness was grueling. It's not for the weak and faint-hearted. The process of humility and healing was a long one. Through my four years of college, I constantly battled with pride and letting go of my hurts from the past. Sometimes I would allow myself or the enemy to pull me back into those hurtful experiences, and I would stumble up the mountain. But then, I remembered who my God was and who I was. I did not want to be caged by pride, and I didn't want chains of anger, bitterness, hurt, and sadness wrapped around my heart. I allowed God to fill my heart with His love, grace, and forgiveness. He was the one who allowed me to bring myself low, but He was the one to bring me to the top with my whole being surrendering to Him.

God tested my heart to see where it was at. Looking at Deuteronomy 8:2 one more time, we see the word "heart," "Remember how the Lord your God led you all the way in the wilderness these forty years, to humble and test you in order to know what was in your heart, whether or not you would keep his commands." So far, we have covered the words "remember," "wilderness," and "humble," but now I want to focus on the heart. In this scripture, God wants us to remember how He led us through our wilderness to humble us before Him to search our hearts.

In the first chapter, we talked about our hearts and how everything flows from them. Our emotions, actions, thoughts, and our personalities flow from the heart. That means what we think and what we feel generate who we are and how we will react in situations. In the above example, I had a prideful and a broken heart that guided me along a destructive path. My heart was not rooted in God's Word or His Spirit. It did not have a sure foundation. It was muddy, brown, black, and mixed with all kinds of different materials. None of which could stand the test of trials. As a result, God tested me. He tested my heart to put it on the right course of action.

In Jeremiah 17, we see God doing the same thing He did to me. He was testing people's hearts. These people were worshipping other gods, building altars for their idols, putting their faith in the world, and rejecting God. Sin was running rampant among these people. God spoke through Jeremiah to tell the people, "The heart is deceitful above all things and beyond cure. Who can understand it? I the LORD search the heart and examine the mind, to reward each person according to their conduct, according to what their deeds deserve" (Jeremiah 17:9–10, NIV).

God searches all hearts during our testing. Those whose hearts are not searched will continue to rot. It will continue to burn with anger and hate, keeping our hearts broken. And when the rotting takes over the heart, then the rotting takes over our life. Remember, everything flows from the heart, which flows outward to our life.

If our hearts are flowing with pride and cracking with brokenness, then in our life, we will be prideful and broken at the same time. So, when God enters into our problem, and we are at rock bottom, our hearts are being tested. He seeks to humble us before Him, so our hearts are made new through the humbling experience of the wilderness. And when we become humbled, then our hearts become rooted in God. Read what God spoke to Jeremiah,

> But blessed is the one who trusts in the LORD, whose confidence is in him. They will be like a tree planted by the water that sends out its roots by the stream. It does not fear when heat comes; its leaves are always green. It has no worries in a year of drought and never fails to bear fruit.
>
> Jeremiah 17:7–8 (NIV)

Our humbled hearts will be able to withstand the test of trials, the healing process of brokenness, and reject the pride that tries to enter. Our downfall is the prideful heart, but the humbled heart is the restoration of life.

Let us now turn our attention to Deuteronomy 8:3 (NIV), "He humbled you, causing you to hunger and then feeding you with manna, which neither you nor your ancestors had known, to teach you that man does not live on bread alone but on every word that comes from the mouth of the LORD." In this scripture, we see what God did for the Israelites in the wilderness. Not only did He humble them through the wilderness by testing them to see what was in the heart, but He also provided them with manna. Though this manna was real, and they did consume it, it was also symbolic of the Word of God. The Israelites did not live on sustenance alone, but only on the Word of God did the Israelites have victory in their wilderness.

Manna literally means "what is it?" (Exodus 16:15, NIV). When the Israelites saw it on the ground, their first exclamation was, "What is it?" Then Moses said, "It is the bread the LORD has given you to eat" (Exodus 16:15, NIV). Manna was sweet like honey, spiced with coriander just like the Word of God. Moses implied this. He knew the manna had a double meaning. We see this when Jesus said,

> Whoever eats my flesh and drinks my blood remains in me, and I in them. Just as the living Father sent me and I live because of the Father, so the one who feeds on me will live because of me. This is the bread that came down from heaven. Your ancestors ate manna and died, but whoever feeds on this bread will live forever.
>
> John 6:56–58 (NIV)

Jesus is the Living Word of God. Thus, when we apply His Word to our wilderness and our hearts, then understanding comes—an understanding of why we are walking through the wilderness in the first place. The Word also convicts us of the pride within while humbling us in the process. This is our manna. Once we get a taste of God's Word and see how it applies in our circumstances, then we hunger for more. We hunger for manna.

As we come to know His Word as our survival, then our brokenness becomes no more. Living on His Word has no room for brokenness. Brokenness is no more our identity, but God's Word is (Ephesians 1 and 2). We are His children, who He loves so much that He gave His one and only Son to be sacrificed on the cross. We do not eat manna to fill the cracks of a broken heart, but we eat manna to transform, heal, and redeem our hearts fully.

If we just eat manna to fill the cracks, then we are still prideful in our hearts. We are still broken. We only want to eat half of the manna because it is what we want. We want only the good of our healing, forgiveness, and redemption. We don't want the other half that convicts us of the offense we hold onto against the people who hurt us or the world. The other half is our hard walk in the wilderness towards trusting and surrendering to God for our full healing, full forgiveness, and full redemption. When we reject eating the hard part of the manna, our hearts are still prideful because we think that only by our ways can we be fully healed, fully forgiven, and fully redeemed. Only when we eat our manna in full are we transformed into something new. God's Word says, "Therefore, if anyone is in Christ, the new creation has come: The old has gone, the new is here!" (2 Corinthians 5:17, NIV).

As we eat our full manna, transforming from something old to new, our pride starts to slip away, replacing it with selflessness. An understanding comes that "The Lord is close to the broken-hearted and saves those who are crushed in spirit" (Psalm 34:18, NIV). Though God does let us fall when we become prideful, He always picks us back up and saves us from death itself. When we are broken and crushed by others or the things of this world or the difficult walk through the wilderness, God takes delight in us. We become humbled by our experiences. God says, "I live in a high and holy place, but also with the one who is contrite and lowly in spirit, to revive the spirit of the lowly and to revive the heart of the contrite" (Isaiah 57:15, NIV). Our downfall is the start of a new beginning.

CHAPTER 5

Surrender

*"Do not conform to the pattern of this world, but be transformed
by the renewing of your mind. Then you will be able to test and
approve what God's will is—his good, pleasing and perfect will"*
(Romans 12:2, NIV).

As we encounter the pridefulness of our broken hearts through the
wilderness, we must conquer this sin and navigate our hearts back
to God. To accomplish this, we must surrender our whole beings
to God. This surrendering is one of heart, body, and soul. It will
bring healing, forgiveness, and restoration to the broken heart.

In the previous chapter, we talked about what happens during
our brokenness when we go through a wilderness that is bare
and treacherous. We must go through this wilderness to shed off
the brokenness of our hearts. Sometimes during this wilderness,
instead of letting God mold our hearts back together, we tend
to want to do that ourselves. By doing it ourselves, pride will
enter the heart, a prideful spirit that screams for validation of
ourselves. Instead of walking through the wilderness to heal our
cracked hearts, we now have to walk through the wilderness to
be humbled and healed. It becomes a long and arduous journey.
During our walk in the wilderness, we are reminded that God has
provided for us regardless of us becoming prideful. Our duty is to
grab hold of that provision, a provision that is sweet-tasting—the

provision of manna. We must eat this manna fully. For if we only eat it halfway, then we are not fully trusting in God, but if we eat it fully, then our prideful broken hearts will become transformed into something new.

Yet, we can only eat this manna fully when we surrender wholly to God. This scripture, Romans 12:2 (NIV), tells us exactly how to eat our manna fully and surrender to God, "Do not conform to the pattern of this world, but be transformed by the renewing of your mind. Then you will be able to test and approve what God's will is—his good, pleasing and perfect will." To surrender, we must: 1) not conform to the ways, thoughts, and actions of this world; 2) be transformed by the renewing of our minds, and; 3) our hearts will know the will of God, which is good, pleasing, and perfect.

Let's talk about our first hurdle to surrendering to God. There is no way around this. If we want our broken hearts to become healed and redeemed, then we cannot let our hearts become corrupted. That means we cannot let our hearts stay prideful or sinful in any way. We cannot conform to this world. Remember when Adam and Eve committed the first sin, which started a ripple effect for eternity? Well, that first sin has been imprinted on us since the day we were born. It is inevitable. We cannot escape sin until we have been taken up into heaven. But we can repent of any sin and be cleansed because of the shedding of Jesus' blood at the cross. His blood is what cleanses us daily when we repent sincerely. This is the Good News, and we must not become slack. Even when we repent sincerely, we can still be tempted by the ways of this world. The ways of the world are ruled by Satan himself, the great tempter.

So, the question is, how do we not conform to this world if we are constantly at battle with the temptations of our hearts?

Simple. We surrender to Jesus Christ, who died specifically for us so we can be set free from this world.

Before I delve further into our answer, I want to first talk about the world we live in. The world we live in is only a temporary resting place. While we are here, we are meant to spread the Good News and glorify God through all that we do. We are waiting for the return of Jesus, and while we wait, God is preparing us for His return. He is strengthening our faith for the end of times that will happen. But often in this world, we encounter hurts, pains, brokenness, and an otherworldly battle. We get knocked off the course God has set for us. If we allow it, this world will crush us. It will break our hearts, and we will become unrighteous before God. In Ephesians, Paul wrote what happens when we allow the world to take hold of our hearts and let the ruler of the world reign over us.

> As for you, you were dead in your transgressions and sins, in which you used to live when you followed the ways of this world and of the ruler of the kingdom of the air, the spirit who is now at work in those who are disobedient. All of us also lived among them at one time, gratifying the cravings of our flesh and following its desires and thoughts. Like the rest, we were by nature deserving of wrath.
>
> Ephesians 2:1–3 (NIV)

This world opposes anything that is of God. That means you and me. We are God's creation, and we were meant to live in harmony with everything He created, but when Satan fell from heaven, he became ruler of this world. He causes havoc and is in opposition to you. But God sent someone who would free you and redeem you. He sent your Advocator, your Warrior, and your Prince of Peace. He sent Jesus.

Jesus is our answer to everything. Jesus is our Healer to our broken hearts. He is our shield from the temptations of this world. His blood is the purifier for our sinful hearts. When we surrender to Him, our hearts no longer beat with the blood of a sinner, but they beat with the blood of a Redeemer. God's greatest gift to us is His Son. The gift was bought because of God's grace and mercy. He did not have to let His Son be sacrificed for us. We don't deserve it. But because of His great grace and mercy, Jesus became the blood sacrifice that Adam and Eve could never give. Jesus forgives, cleanses, purifies, and erases all of our sins. That includes the hurts, pains, pride, and offenses. In Colossians 1:15–19, we truly see the gift of Jesus.

> The Son is the image of the invisible God, the firstborn over all creation. For in him all things were created: things in heaven and on earth, visible and invisible, whether thrones or powers or rulers or authorities; all things have been created through him and for him. He is before all things, and in him all things hold together. And he is the head of the body, the church; he is the beginning and the firstborn from among the dead, so that in everything he might have the supremacy. For God was pleased to have all his fullness dwell in him.

> Colossians 1:15–19 (NIV)

Surrendering wholly to Jesus makes our hearts holy. When our hearts are holy, then the temptations of our hearts no longer become temptations. They do not satisfy us anymore. Only Jesus can satisfy us.

Placing our hearts in the palm of Jesus' hands conquers this world. Only when we take our hearts into our own hands will we start to conform to this world. That is when the hurts, pains, and anger start to build up. Our hearts will become broken when we do it ourselves, when we try to heal on our own, when we try to forgive on our own, and when we try to redeem our broken hearts on our own. Being independent of Jesus is conforming to the world. But when we become dependent upon Him, then we will be set free from our broken hearts and this world.

Let me tell you a story from my past. As I have mentioned numerous times, the two years I spent with my father changed me drastically. I became damaged. I carried around the hurt like a weapon. I lashed out at people who tried to help and said hurtful words to my family, who showed me unconditional love. Yet, I knew they weren't to blame. Instead, I blamed the only one who was trying to enter my heart, God. I questioned Him severely, I blamed Him for allowing bad things to happen to me, and I was beginning to hate Him for it.

Yet, even when He knew my thoughts of Him, He was still penetrating the walls that I erected around my heart. He still wanted me to come to Him. He kept loving me unconditionally. I was too stubborn, too hurt, and too prideful to see it, to see Him working in my heart.

Holding this strong offense against God was crushing me. I was carrying hurt, anger, and hate in my heart that was weighing me down greatly. I was letting the world's view conform to me. I wasn't surrendering towards God wholly; that was leaving my heart open for the world's conformity. My heart was becoming more broken than it already was. And God, He kept forgiving me, He kept loving me, and kept protecting me from my father and the enemy. I didn't deserve any of it. After all, I put the blame upon His shoulders. What's more shameful is I was going to church all the while I was blaming Him. How hypocritical of me. But I am thankful that I kept going to church because something inside of me knew I needed Him. Something inside of me wanted to love God the way He loved me. Something inside of me needed God to change who I was. Something inside of me didn't want to keep blaming God; I didn't want to keep living this way. I didn't want what the world had to offer to heal my hurt and broken heart.

Then there was this one night at church. This one night, I couldn't handle my heart being broken. This one night, I was ready to give up. I wanted to stop fighting. But this one night at church, God saved me. I don't recall what was preached that night, but I do recall the altar call. Before I went down there, there was a church member who offered multiple times before if I wanted to go down to the altar, but I always said no. I was fearful of going down because I knew that the Holy Spirit would convict me greatly of my sins. Honestly, I was fearful of God.

I am thankful that the Holy Spirit prompted me to go down that night because God saved me. He did not punish me. Though He did convict me of my sins and brought understanding to my eyes, He also forgave me. That night I was prayed over, and the fear that was coursing through my heart was taken away and replaced with a reverence fear of God. My heart became healed that night of brokenness. My heart was placed back together, but it did have scars, and it would take me a few years to be completely and wholly healed. But it was melded back together with the love and forgiveness of God.

Only when I was at my breaking point did I fully surrender to God. And that surrendering healed me. It brought my brokenness to a close. Though that night was a joyous one, it was also a sad one. I only chose to surrender when I had no other choice. Only when my strategies and self-help were exhausted did I look towards God. Understand this—it's very important—never does God want to be last; He wants to be first. He wants us to choose Him first. With that being said, we must not wait till our breaking point, like I did, to surrender to God. We must surrender to Him every single day, every single hour, every single minute, and every single second. If we do not surrender to Him, then our hearts are not fully aligned with Him. They are still aligned with this world. Surrendering takes an act of complete devotion and obedience only to God. It is giving up all you know, even your life, and following only God. It is going against the values, beliefs, and customs of this world. Surrendering to God is our freedom from our brokenness.

Once we have made the decision not to conform to this world and we have decided to fight against the temptations of our hearts, the second hurdle we need to jump over is being transformed by the Lord, a transformation that is of our minds. The renewal of our minds leads to the renewal of our hearts. Our transformation comes from our Lord Jesus Christ. When we invite Him into our hearts, then we are inviting Him to completely transform our hearts. We undergo character development. Instead of thinking world-like, we start to think God-like. The Apostle Paul says, "And we all, who with unveiled faces contemplate the Lord's glory, are being transformed into his image with ever-increasing glory, which comes from the Lord, who is the Spirit" (2 Corinthians 3:18, NIV).

Evermore, we are being transformed into the image of God. When we were conformed to this world, our spirits were full of sin, but when we surrender to God, our spirits are renewed to their original glory. The original glory that Adam and Eve experienced before they sinned. A connectedness and oneness with God that no enemy or the flesh could ever disrupt. It is that same original glory that was Jesus. He is the perfect image of God. By one simple act, His act of sacrifice, Jesus made it possible for us to be transformed. When He sacrificed His body on the cross, then rose three days later, He made it possible for us to be transformed by the renewal of our minds. He embodies transformation and renewal.

Look at it this way, for us to be transformed and renewed, we also need to sacrifice our bodies on the cross. Let me clarify: we need to sacrifice our old bodies on the cross. Our old bodies are the sins we committed, following the world's ways and brokenness. Once that act is done, we are telling God we fully surrender to Him just like Jesus did. After we rise from our graves and shed off our old bodies, we are then resurrected in our new bodies. The Apostle Paul explains this transformation better in the Book of Romans.

> For if we have been united with him in a death like his, we will certainly also be united with him in a resurrection like his. For we know that our old self was crucified with him so that the body ruled by sin might be done away with, that we should no longer be slaves to sin—because anyone who has died has been set free from sin. Now if we died with Christ, we believe that we will also live with him.
>
> Romans 6:5–8 (NIV)

So, the question is, what does transformation have to do with surrendering to God and brokenness? The answer: it has everything to do with surrendering to God and brokenness. When we surrender to God, we obey God no matter what, even at the cost of our own life. Surrendering to God means doing His will above our will, dropping what we think we need, and letting Him have control over every aspect of our lives. Once we surrender, then we transform. This transformation is a shedding of our old lives, which is shedding off our brokenness, hate, anger, and sadness, then putting on our new lives. Once our transformation is complete, we have a new heart, and we are in harmony with God.

During the process of transformation, we constantly have to surrender ourselves to God because, during that time, we will be tempted by this world and the enemy. Even still, when the transformation is complete, we will go through trials and tribulations. It is how our faith grows in God. After our transformation, it is not just a bed of roses and perfection. No, we will have to fight against the temptations of our hearts, fight against the enemy, and go through trials to strengthen our minds, heart, and faith in God.

To live in harmony with God is to surrender your life to God. To be transformed by the freedom of giving up your life to God. Your life is in His hands. He will never leave you, forsake you, or destroy you. Rather, being transformed in His image is following all of His decrees and commands with total obedience. In the Book of Ezekiel, God spoke to His people, saying, "I will give them an undivided heart and put a new spirit in them; I will remove from them their heart of stone and give them a heart of flesh. Then they will follow my decrees and be careful to keep my laws. They will be my people, and I will be their God (Ezekiel 11:19–20, NIV). With this obedience comes the glory of the Lord that becomes our transformation by the renewing of our minds and hearts. Brokenness no longer steals God's glory. For renewal sings our name.

Once we have overcome this world and let God transform our hearts, then we will be able to test God's will in our lives. By testing, I mean if we are doing our will or His good, pleasing, and perfect will. Throughout our lives, we will continuously test what the will of God is, and in turn, we will be tested by God to obey His will. When God tests us, it is to determine our character and our spiritual standing. Thus, when we go through our wilderness, during our brokenness, that is God testing us to strengthen our trust and faith in Him. We are being tested to be strong spiritually. To finally surrender and obey His will for our lives during our brokenness.

God's will is revealed in pieces as we become more mature in our relationship with Him. Our maturity comes from the testing of our obedience to Him. The testing is if we will surrender to His will or surrender to our will. When we choose God's will and are fully obedient to Him, then we must surrender all the brokenness within us. If we hold onto our brokenness, then we are not fully invested in God's will. We are still holding onto our pride; we are holding onto our will. Then, if we are still holding onto our pride, we are being conformed to this world. By being conformed to this world, we cannot be transformed by God. We must surrender to God's will because then we will be healed, forgiven, and redeemed from our broken hearts.

God leaves the choice up to us. He gives us free will. Choose His will or choose our will. Once you choose God's will, I need you to understand that though God's will is good, pleasing, and perfect, you will encounter suffering along the way. Some of this suffering will be during your wilderness, but the suffering will be necessary for you to be healed, forgiven, and redeemed from your brokenness. This suffering will not crush you; instead, it will build you up and grow you in your relationship with God. We must view our suffering with joy in our hearts because that means we are being tested by God to grow spiritually. James, the half-brother of Jesus, says, "Consider it pure joy, my brothers and sisters, whenever you face trials of many kinds, because you know that the testing of your faith produces perseverance. Let perseverance finish its work so that you may be mature and complete, not lacking anything" (James 1:2–4, NIV). Suffering from God and having our faith tested is a sure way of knowing we are in the will of God.

The suffering is inevitable, but our response to the suffering will build us up or break us down. God's will is not for the faint of heart. Our suffering will build us up if we surrender wholeheartedly to God and trust that He will protect, provide, and fight for us. But our suffering will break us down if we become bitter, blameful towards God, and more heartbroken than we already were. So, choosing God's will brings abundance and joy, but it will also bring the suffering that matures our faith.

Looking at the verse of Romans 12:2 (NIV), "Do not conform to the pattern of this world, but be transformed by the renewing of your mind. Then you will be able to test and approve what God's will is—his good, pleasing, and perfect will," we can now understand the importance of surrendering wholly to God. For us to surrender, we must not conform to the world's ways; we must be transformed by Jesus, letting Him renew our minds and hearts, and after our transformation, we will be able to test the will of God, knowing it is good, pleasing, and perfect. This leads to wholly surrendering our broken hearts to God. Once we surrender our brokenness, then God can heal and redeem our hearts. But more importantly, forgiveness will be present in our hearts, and our relationship with God will mature.

Let this scripture be planted in your heart, "But seek first his kingdom and his righteousness, and all these things will be given to you as well" (Matthew 6:33, NIV). Seeking His kingdom first is giving over our pride and brokenness to Him. Your heart matters to Him. Therefore, surrender all and be healed, forgiven, and redeemed.

SECTION 3

FORGIVE

CHAPTER 6

Scars

"Help us, God our Savior, for the glory of your name; deliver us and forgive our sins for your name's sake" (Psalm 79:9, NIV).

So far, we have talked about our brokenness. More specifically, the impact brokenness has on our hearts and how we can become broken. When we become broken, our hearts become susceptible to a prideful heart, especially when we have to walk through our wilderness. This pride and brokenness is a deadly combination that will cause our downfall. Though when we do fall, it is because God is humbling us and putting us back together.

Our eyes need to be set on Him. Once our eyes are set on Him, we must turn our broken hearts to Him. Turning our broken hearts to Him is called surrendering. Surrendering all that we are, the broken parts and the best parts. Only when we surrender all, not holding back one ounce, will it lead to our heart's forgiveness, healing, and redemption.

In this section, we will talk about forgiveness. Throughout, forgiveness will be a prevalent theme while we navigate our scars, our cracks, and our fulfillment in forgiveness. Before I get into this chapter and the scripture that goes with this chapter, I want to first talk about forgiveness. Specifically, what is forgiveness, and what happens when we forgive.

Merriam Webster defines to forgive as "to cease to feel resentment against (an offender)."[6] It is a verb in which there is an action that must take place for the word to have meaning. Forgiveness is the stoppage of harboring sinful emotions and accusations such as hate, anger, or blame. Forgiveness takes place when the one who was hurt initiates the first step of reconciliation towards the other person or God, for the broken to have the heart to forgive needs also to be forgiven for their actions. This is only accomplished through God.

First and foremost, God is the source of all forgiveness. We see this through Jesus Christ. Because of His sacrifice and the blood that flowed from Him, we are cleansed and forgiven from all sins, no matter how egregious (Colossians 1:21–22). For us to be forgiven, we must repent with sincerity and humility. Let's look at the story of Jacob and Esau in the Book of Genesis. Jacob and Esau were brothers, and their parents were Isaac and Rebekah. Esau was a skilled hunter, and Jacob liked to hang around his home. One day when Esau came back from his hunt, he was famished. Meanwhile, Jacob was making stew, and when Esau saw this, he asked for some stew. Instead of giving Esau stew, Jacob wanted an exchange. Esau could have the stew if he gave Jacob his birthright. So, that was what Esau did. He gave his birthright up in exchange for some stew.

What sets this whole story up is the relationship the parents had with the brothers. Isaac favored Esau, and Rebekah favored Jacob. Isaac was an old man and dying. Before he died, he wanted to give a blessing to his oldest son, Esau. But first, he asked his son to go hunting and make his favorite stew. While Isaac was speaking with Esau, Rebekah was eavesdropping. She told Jacob to make Isaac's favorite stew while Esau was gone. Then tricked

Isaac into thinking that Jacob was Esau, which resulted in stealing the blessing that was first promised to Esau. So, that is what Jacob did, and Isaac blessed him. Therefore, Esau didn't just sell his birthright, but his blessing was taken away by Jacob. Because of the injustice done to him, Esau held resentment, anger, and hate against Jacob.

Jacob fled from Esau, going on a journey in which he traversed through many tribulations that turned his heart more towards God. One of Jacob's journeys took him back towards his brother, Esau. When Jacob crossed over into Esau's territory, he was initially fearful for his life and remorseful that he took his brother's birthright and blessing. One night in his brother's territory, God got ahold of Jacob's heart. In turn, Jacob asked for forgiveness from God, and then when he met with his brother, he asked for forgiveness. Only when Jacob's heart was ready, and he was humbled, did God forgive him. This encouraged Jacob to ask for forgiveness from Esau. Because Jacob was sincere and humble in his repentance, God forgave.

Now, if Jacob were still prideful and only repented in spite of Esau, then God would bring judgment on him. Possibly, God would not have passed the mantle that He first gave Abraham and then to Jacob's father, Isaac. Always come to God asking forgiveness with humility and sincerity.

As a brokenhearted person, you cannot harbor hate or anger against the thing that caused the brokenness. You cannot harbor bitterness or blame towards God. The forgiveness that you seek from God will not be true forgiveness. It will be false forgiveness because, in your heart, you have not forgiven the thing that hurt you.

As Christians, we are to forgive all who have hurt us. If we do not, then God will not forgive us for our sins. Jesus emphasized this point in Matthew 6:14–15 (NIV), "For if you forgive other people when they sin against you, your heavenly Father will also forgive you. But if you do not forgive others their sins, your Father will not forgive your sins." We cannot use our brokenness as an excuse to not forgive others.

I cannot stress this enough; we must forgive others who have caused us pain because if we don't, then this unforgiveness will break our hearts more, almost to the point that it stays broken forever. When the heart stays broken, our relationship with God will become broken also. A broken relationship is not a healthy relationship, and a broken relationship is a one-sided relationship. When our relationship with God is broken, we tend to blame Him for our pain, becoming increasingly bitter towards Him, and we close off our hearts from Him. This broken relationship will not help you in any way. When we show unforgiveness, we are missing out on God's blessings, grace, mercy, healing, and love.

Having unforgiveness is like a slap to the face of Jesus. He forgave you when you didn't deserve it. He sacrificed Himself for you so that you could receive His grace and mercy in full. Do not reject the gift that Jesus has already purchased for you. You are to "bear with each other and forgive one another if any of you has a grievance against someone. Forgive as the Lord forgave you" (Colossians 3:13, NIV). Jesus commands us to forgive seventy times seven. We can't just forgive those who have hurt us once, but we must forgive over and over again. It will not take one time to forgive for a broken heart to be made right again. Rather, it will take forgiving numerous times for the heart to be put back together. It will take seventy times seven.

Once we choose to forgive those who have caused us pain with all our hearts in sincerity and humility, we turn to ask God for forgiveness. He will examine and judge the heart if it's right or not. Once our hearts are right, then God will forgive us for our anger, hate, bitterness, and blame. No longer is our relationship with God broken but restored (Colossians 1:21–22). The forgiveness that we give others, and the forgiveness that we receive from God, turn our hearts from broken to scarred. Our hearts start to meld themselves together, forming into scars.

Scars are something else in their entirety. When we are injured, and our injury is deep enough in our skin that as it heals, a scar will more than likely be present. The scar reminds us of that injury. Some people think scars are cool to have on the skin, and others see it as a disgrace, ruining their beauty or perfection. I think our scars remind us of what we have overcome in our past. These scars hurt when they start to heal, and when they form, they can be vicious-looking. Sometimes we become embarrassed of those vicious scars, but we should never feel the shame of the wounds we have overcome. They are our testimony of what God has done for us.

Our scars are formed when we first forgive the ones who hurt us and then ask forgiveness from God. For us to forgive, we need to initiate that first contact. We must cry out to the Lord our Savior, asking for His help. We cannot forgive on our terms but only on His. By His strength, can we then forgive. In the Strong's Concordance, the Hebrew word for help is *azar* meaning, "to help, assist, aid."[7] When we cry out for God to help us in our forgiveness, we are asking Him to assist and aid us in that venture. We are asking Him for His strength, His confidence, His mercy, and grace to help us. Forgiving people on our terms will never heal us the correct way. Our wounds will still be open and might become infected because we are still holding onto bitterness, anger, and hate. Doing it our way will cause our hearts to be more broken.

God's way will always lead to full healing. Crying out for help is the start of the healing process that results in scars. Don't leave the wounds open for infection. Choose to set your pride aside and cry out for help to the Lord.

Read these words, "I lift up my eyes to the mountains—where does my help come from? My help comes from the Lord, the Maker of heaven and earth" (Psalm 121:1–2, NIV). Lift your eyes to the one who sits on the throne, for He is your helper. He is your Healer, and He will close those gaping wounds. Though you can't physically see God working, He is ever-present. He is present by the Holy Spirit. God sent His Holy Spirit to be an advocate for you, a comforter, and a counselor. The Holy Spirit knows all of you. He knows the emotions, the hurts, and the state of the heart. The Holy Spirit is within you as a constant presence of God that is a constant presence of help in forgiveness. Jesus tells His disciples this, "And I will ask the Father, and he will give you another advocate to help you and be with you forever—the Spirit of truth. The world cannot accept him, because it neither sees him nor knows him. But you know him, for he lives with you and will be in you" (John 14:16–17, NIV). Daughters and sons of God, because the Holy Spirit is with you, God is in you. He is a constant presence with you. He is giving you His strength and wisdom to forgive. He is forming those scars this very second.

God is not only the helper of our scars; He is our Savior. He saves us. When we can't bear our wounds anymore, crying out for help, He saves. God doesn't merely save us to be saved. He saves us to be forgiven, healed, redeemed, and loved. Yes, His saving is full of love. A love for us that was bought with a steep price. It was the sacrifice of His Son on the cross and the thick blood that ran out of His veins.

For he chose us in him before the creation of the world to be holy and blameless in his sight. In love he predestined us for adoption to sonship through Jesus Christ, in accordance with his pleasure and will—to the praise of his glorious grace, which he has freely given us in the One he loves.

Ephesians 1:4–6 (NIV)

Only the Lord is the Savior of our brokenness. Once we accept that fact, then our wounds start to heal into scars, even though accepting the Savior will not be easy. Our pride will become an obstacle, and we will want to heal our wounds our way. These earthly bodies want the world's healing ways, in which they will fight against God's ways. We must push through the fleshly desires to accept our Savior. Set pride aside and be humble in accepting the Lord.

Once the decision has been made, then the healing process starts, and scars start to form. The healing process will be grueling and sore. It will not be an easy feat. There will be lots of crying, yelling, and an inner struggle that only you will experience. So, trust and have faith in the Savior that He will save you no matter how deep the wounds are or how gruesome they look. He will turn those deep and gruesome wounds into healing, beautiful scars.

As God begins to save us from our brokenness, He desires to be glorified. Truthfully, our wounds that turned into scars weren't accomplished by our healing but by His healing did they turn into scars. We must praise and glorify Him for all the healing. Understand this: God is glory; thus, when we give Him the glory, we are then glory itself because we were created in His image. Now, we are not the glory that God is, but we are a small portion of His glory. These scars that we have are not only meant to be a sign of healing, but they are a testament to the glory of God. The glory of God enters into these scars, and all will know who sits on the throne of our hearts. He needs to enter our closed-off hearts for His glory to be present in our brokenness. In Psalm 24:7–10, the psalmist describes who the King of glory is in our hearts.

> Lift up your heads, you gates; be lifted up, you ancient doors, that the King of glory may come in. Who is this King of glory? The LORD strong and mighty, the LORD mighty in battle. Lift up your heads, you gates; lift them up, you ancient doors, that the King of glory may come in. Who is he, this King of glory? The LORD Almighty— he is the King of glory.

Psalm 24:7–10 (NIV)

Our hearts are like the ancient doors that need to be lifted. We cannot let our wounds keep our hearts closed off forever. We will not grow as a person, and we will not grow in our relationship with God. Don't be an ancient door that hasn't been pried open for centuries. Inside those doors are dustiness, the old things of the past, brokenness, and darkness. Lift your head and open those ancient doors to the beautiful glory of the Lord Almighty. Even when you think it's too hard to open the doors, understand that God already opened it for you when His Son came out of the tomb. He's already helping you even before you knew you needed help. With an open heart, read this scripture, "We were therefore buried with him through baptism into death in order that, just as Christ was raised from the dead through the glory of the Father, we too may live a new life" (Romans 6:4, NIV).

As Christ is in you, so the glory of God is raising you from the death of a broken heart, bringing a new life that is full of His glory, presence, and joy. When it comes to our wounded hearts, pleading to be healed by God, we must not see with our fleshly eyes. We must see with our spiritual eyes because when we do, then we can see our hearts turn from wounded to scarred; that brings glory to God. Eventually, scars disappear, and they will become a shadow of the past, but our wounded hearts will last forever. Don't let your wounded heart become your eternal destination.

Letting the glory of God reign in our hearts brings forgiveness to us. This forgiveness is the healing process of our wounds. Let me tell you a story of my heart's experience. During the two years I lived with my father, my parents were separated. At the end of the two years, my mom came back from Washington State, and by then, I had already gone through emotional and mental turmoil. So, I decided that I would go live with my mom. This decision was the start of my healing heart.

When I was living with my mom, I was introduced to God. From there, my journey to forgiveness started. I learned quickly that God didn't want my heart to be bitter, hateful, and angry at my father. He wanted me to forgive him and to love him as He loved me. Every time God would impress this on my heart, I would reject it. I didn't want to forgive. I didn't want to be vulnerable again. I thought if I didn't forgive, then I'd be protecting myself from more hurt. But what I didn't realize was the more I rejected what God wanted me to do, the more my heart kept breaking. I was spiraling into the darkness of bitterness, hate, and anger. The only way my heart could heal was if I forgave my father, God's way, and surrendered myself to Him.

Many people in my life urged me to forgive my father, but it was just so hard. I thought it was impossible. So, what I did was constantly say was, "I forgive you," over and over again. I thought that saying those three words would convince my heart to accept it and bring healing. Even then, that didn't work because, in my heart, there was still that bitterness, anger, and hate towards him. For years I went through this cycle of fake forgiveness. I was stuck. My relationship with God wasn't growing, I wasn't growing as a person, and my relationship with the people I love the most wasn't growing. Because I couldn't forgive with sincerity, humility, and love, I didn't trust the people closest to me, and I didn't trust God. I started to blame God for my problems, and I started to push others away. I closed my heart up more. And to be frank, it was exhausting. I was tired of going through the cycle, and I was tired of being stuck. I was tired of protecting my heart on my own. I was tired of being bitter, angry, and hateful. I was tired of crying. I was tired of the person I was.

Remember that story I told you a couple of chapters ago about the night I went to church? That night changed everything. Well, that night was the night I was done with running away; I was done being unforgiving. That night all I needed was God to change me. Change my heart, dry up my tears, and heal my wounds. I needed God. And that night, I surrendered all. I chose to forgive my father for all he did to me and for all the hurt that I endured. When the choice was made to forgive sincerely, humbly, and with God's love, I was set free. God was starting to heal my heart. The road to forgiving my father was not short. I forgave him a little at a time, and because of that, I could ask God for forgiveness. It would take me years to forgive my father fully and for my cracks to start to scar. Those same scars took time to disappear, but God's forgiveness lasts forever.

He was always there for me in my darkest time, shining a light for me to see His path. Never did He cause me pain; rather, He wanted me to face my greatest fear and pain with Him by my side.

He was my rock, my strength, and my provider. Surrendering solely to Him and forgiving my father grew my relationship with God and the people close to me. I finally became unstuck, no longer living in the past. My heart could sing a new tune: freedom.

CHAPTER 7

Cracks

*"It is for freedom that Christ has set us free. Stand firm, then,
and do not let yourselves be burdened again by a yoke of slavery"
(Galatians 5:1, NIV).*

As our hearts start to scar, inevitably, there will still be cracks
visible. These are the cracks that forgiveness cannot heal. These
cracks are the ones only God can reveal to us, and only God can
heal with our full surrender. The two cracks we will discover are
worthiness and identity.

Let's turn our focus over to worthiness, or shall I say worthlessness. When the heart starts to scar, a different layer of the heart
unveils—the unveiling of worthlessness. Worthlessness is wrought
from how we view ourselves because of the hurt, pain, hate, bitterness,
and anger we went through. We have lost our sense of worth. Our
sense of worth is the value we see in ourselves and the value we bring
to others. To be frank, this is an egocentric view. It's a self-view, a
view of how the world sees us. This view hinders us from truly being
set free from all of our cracks. If all we see is that our worth equates
to how we view ourselves and how we view ourselves is through the
lens of others, then we will be stuck in our worthlessness. Our hearts
will not be properly healed, and the forgiveness we have worked so
hard to accomplish will be for nothing.

This brings us to the conclusion that our worth only comes from God, not from ourselves or the world. He is the only one to see us as worthy, and we are to look up to the worthiness. Even when we don't deserve this worthiness, He still shows us the grace and mercy of it.

Let me tell you a story of someone else's worthiness journey. This journey is about a woman who, at birth, was given no name. Even when she was growing up, she was given no name, and her childhood was tough. Her mother worked long hours, and the hours she did have left in the day were spent sleeping from the hard work she endured. Yet, somehow her mother developed a string of broken and abusive relationships with men while her daughter watched her every move. The child spent a lot of her time with her grandmother and her friends. To say the least, though her mother provided for all her necessities and did love her greatly, this child was on her own. Sometimes she got into trouble with her friends, and sometimes she would spend hours with her grandmother, her rock. Her grandmother kept her in check and even brought her to church. But as the child started to become a woman, an adult in her own right, she met a man named Tsalmaveth (*tsal-maw-veth*), which in Hebrew means shadow or death.[8] A relationship was formed with the shadow man, and they became married, joined as one.

At first, they were happy, just a fleeting emotion, but the woman sensed something wrong. Gradually, Tsalmaveth revealed his true heart. He became controlling, emotionally draining, mentally abusive, and at times physically abusive. He became so controlling that he moved her to a caged house far away in the country. When he exerted his power, she saw his black heart and the shadows in his eyes. She endured much at his words. She was tired of living. Her heart was broken and cracked. She was suffocating by the shadows that surrounded her. All she could see were gray and black hues that made up her world.

To escape Tsalmaveth, even for just a few hours, she threw herself into her work, where she succeeded beyond what Tsalmaveth could ever do. Every night when she would come home, he became jealous of her success and beat her back down to the ground with his words. He made sure that she never thought of herself better than the words he said. One night when they were fighting, he asked her, "What is your name?" She responded with no outward emotion but with a heartbreaking, "I am Belial. My name is Belial, meaning worthlessness and hopeless ruin."[9] The woman who was given no name at birth became a woman named Belial. She believed her name to be true that all through her life, she saw herself as worthless.

She was Belial and tired of living. She thought, *What more could happen to me? My life has become nothing. It is not even worth living.* In her desperate plea for help, she recalled all of her good memories, and only a few came. Those few were of her grandmother, her rock. She remembered the times she went to church and how her heart lurched for more of what she heard. She remembered the pastor talking about God and Jesus, how you only have to call His name with sincerity and humility, and He will hear. After all other options were exhausted, during her last desperate plea for help, she cried out to God. She poured her whole heart into Him and asked Him to save her. Save her from her broken heart. Save her from her marriage. Save her from her worthlessness. She cried out to Him for hours. And in that desperate plea, she felt Him. She felt His presence as she welcomed Him wholly. That very moment God changed her heart. His presence entered in.

He became her rock, her guide, her confidence, her courage, her protector, and her provider.

With this changed countenance, the first thing she did was divorce Tsalmaveth. She even marched right to his face and told him, "You are never going to control me again. No longer will I fear you, and no longer will you beat me down with your cruel words!" She held true to her statements, and though at times she wavered, she remembered what her God did for her, what He accomplished through her brokenness. He showed her His unfailing love and His merciful forgiveness. Her heart was slowly healing, and scars were starting to form, but the one place that was struggling to close was the unworthiness she felt she had.

Every day and every night, she would pray to God, "Take my unworthiness away. It is killing a part of my heart." Yet, He could not take it away because she would not give it up. Her unworthiness was what she was used to. She was comfortable holding it inside.

Finally, God said to her, "You cannot hold your unworthiness anymore. I see the hurt you have endured, and every time I see you, I cry for you, My daughter. Let go, My daughter. Let go, for I am giving you a new heart. A heart that will be set free."

With tears in her eyes, she said, "I want to live. I want to live for You. No longer do I want to be caged by Belial. You are my strength, Father. You are my Savior." She became determined to heal her cracked heart. She became absorbed in His Word, she fasted every chance she got, she prayed every day and every night for hours, and she went to church consistently.

Even though her heart was healing from unworthiness, and she understood that her worth was not in others or herself but in God, there was still this feeling of unfinished healing. One day during her prayers, she asked God, "Why is my unworthiness still lingering? I have grown closer to You, and I have almost healed fully. No longer do I fear, no longer am I being controlled, and no longer do words equate to my worth. Why Lord?"

Then, God responded with love, "My daughter, you are My child. Once, you had no name. Then, you called yourself Belial. Your unworthiness still lingers because I have yet to call you by your name. My daughter, your name is Hannah, meaning favored and grace."[10]

At the end of the story, Hannah finally understood what her worth was. Her worth was not found in her name, it was not found in her mother, it was not found in her marriage, and it was not found in the cruel words flung her way. Her worth was found in God. He saw her worthy when she never did. The same goes for our worth. Our worth is not found in others or this world; rather, it is found in God and only God.

I can relate to this woman, Hannah. Except I was born with a name, and my name never changed, but I can relate to her because of the unworthiness she felt in her heart. My father said a lot of hurtful words to me, and sometimes he didn't treat me the way he should have treated his daughter. My father and I bonded over basketball. He taught me how to play, and we would constantly be practicing, helping me be the best basketball player I could be. However, most times, my father pushed me too hard. You know, there is that saying, "Keep pushing to your limits," well, my father pushed me beyond and over my limits.

One of the things he would say to me is, "There is always someone else better than you," which he's right, and it was good motivation, but he would take it as far as I couldn't see my friends or take a vacation. It was constant work, sacrifice, work, sacrifice. I never got a break and never had a social life, so to speak. As a result of that, I became angry, mentally exhausted, and would lash out. There were times when I didn't even want to play basketball anymore because I didn't want to become that person. When I would become angry or push back, he would tell me I was no good or that I wouldn't amount to anything. Even after a game when I didn't play well, he would leave the gym disappointed, and I wouldn't see him for a couple of hours.

The words he would yell at me and the actions he portrayed, I took to heart. I become those words. I saw myself only as worthy as those words. As a result, I struggled with confidence in my basketball career and as a person. Unworthiness was what my heart whispered, especially of God. After I left my father and turned my heart fully to God, I struggled with the notion that God sees everyone as worthy. No matter the sins they have committed, or the hurts they have endured, or the scarred and cracked heart they have, He sees them worthy. Because I was holding on to my unworthiness so tightly, I became cloaked in darkness. Every day I felt as if I was suffocating from this darkness, and it got to the point of me questioning myself, "What is my life worthy of?"

Remember that evening at church I have talked about multiple times? It was that evening that God took this darkness away, and He revealed to me that I am precious to Him, that I am worthy enough for His Son to sacrifice Himself for me. That evening I wasn't healed fully, and I didn't see myself fully worthy of God, but it was a start in the right direction. It has taken me years to finally see my worth in God, and even then, I sometimes doubt. But some scriptures that remind me of my worth are Ephesians 1, 2, and 3. These show me who I am in God. If you are struggling with worthiness, I encourage you to read these chapters every single day and highlight who you are in God.

Just as our worthiness is in God, so is our identity. We cannot let our unworthiness identify who we are. We are loved, cherished, forgiven, chosen, redeemed, provided, protected, and so much more. You are not what others have said, what you have said, or what the enemy has said. Your brokenness and cracks are not your identity. You are what God has said you are. You are "fearfully and wonderfully made" (Psalm 139:14, NIV). Yet, I know that it is hard to let go of your old identity. This is why I want to focus on our chapter scripture, "It is for freedom that Christ has set us free. Stand firm, then, and do not let yourselves be burdened again by a yoke of slavery" (Galatians 5:1, NIV).

To understand and know our identity in God, we first need to know our freedom. Our freedom in God is the start of our identity. Freedom in God is not bondage. People who don't believe in God and live in the world are not free. They are still living in bondage because they have not repented of their sins nor accepted Jesus as their Savior. God wants us to live in the freedom in which He sent His Son to the cross to be sacrificed for us so He could liberate us from bondage.

Our bondage can come in many forms. The bondage we are breaking free from is our unworthiness and lack of identity, which comes from the brokenness we have in our hearts. We cannot be a prisoner of our unworthiness and lack of identity. We will not grow in God, we will not be healed fully, we will not be forgiven properly, and we will not be redeemed to the person God created us to be.

God has provided the escape route. All that needs to be done is to look up at the cross. The Apostle Paul perfectly describes what Christ does for those who are slaves to the world,

Were you a slave when you were called? Don't let it trouble you—although if you can gain your freedom, do so. For the one who was a slave when called to faith in the Lord is the Lord's freed person; similarly, the one who was free when called is Christ's slave. You were bought at a price; do not become slaves of human beings.

1 Corinthians 7:21–23 (NIV)

Once, we were slaves to our unworthiness, our hurts, and our brokenness; now, because of Jesus, we are set free.

When it comes to freedom from our insecurities and our broken hearts, the one question that is often thought or spoken of is "What is my identity?" Sure, we've talked about our identity in the above paragraphs, but we never asked the question. And if we never ask the question, we'll never get the answer. Our identity is rooted in the freedom of Jesus Christ. Some of you may be thinking, *How can that be? This was a man that, during His time, many thought His thinking was radical. And because of that, this ultimately led to Him being shackled, chained, tortured, and crucified.* All of that is true, but for us to be free in Jesus, He first had to become shackled by our sins.

Our bondage is from sin, which leads to other bondages such as unworthiness, lack of identity, and a broken heart. Before Jesus was crucified, we were "a slave to sin" (John 8:34, NIV). After He was crucified when He rose again three days later, we became no longer bound by the sin. His blood atoned for that. "'He himself bore our sins' in his body on the cross, so that we might die to sins and live for righteousness; 'by his wounds, you have been healed'" (1 Peter 2:24, NIV).

The freedom that was purchased by Jesus is not to be abused. He didn't purchase our freedom so we could do whatever we wanted. Rather, He purchased our freedom so that we could live in harmony with God, nurturing our relationship with Him and being the person God created us to be. Before the crucifixion of Jesus, sin kept us chained up, denying us the opportunity or chance to live in harmony with God. As a result, we lived in a chaotic, unharmonized world that muddled our identity in Christ.

We must accept Jesus' death on the cross. As we surrender to Him, the bondage of sin has no power over us. It has no power to define who we are, it has no power to keep us locked up in unworthiness, and it has no power to keep a heart broken. The freedom of not being controlled by sin is liberating to the heart. Your identity is this:

1. you are chosen;
2. you are adopted;
3. you are freed;
4. you are forgiven;
5. you are saved;
6. you are identified by God;
7. you have an everlasting inheritance;
8. you are loved;
9. you are God's masterpiece;
10. you are made new;
11. you are created for a purpose;
12. you are the house/temple God built;
13. you are gifted and talented by God, and;
14. you are God's child.

When we look at this part of the scripture, "It is for freedom that Christ has set us free," we can read it with confidence that, indeed, because of His sacrifice, we are set free. And this freedom reveals that our identity does not lie in bondage, a broken heart, or unworthiness, but it lies in Christ.

Now, let's look at the last part of our chapter scripture, "It is for freedom that Christ has set us free. Stand firm, then, and do not let yourselves be burdened again by a yoke of slavery." Knowing your identity is rested in the freedom that Jesus purchased for you is a victory against the brokenness of your heart. But to stay rested in the freedom, you need to stand firm in that knowledge. To stand means to be in a fixed position, that nothing will budge you, but then when you combine that word with "firm," Merriam Webster's Dictionary defines that as "having a solid or compact structure that resists stress or pressure" and "not easily moved or disturbed."[11] When you stand firm, you are in a position that will not be compromised. You will be in that position no matter what your circumstances are and no matter what pressure is put upon your shoulders.

So, to stand firm in your freedom and identity is crucial to overcoming the brokenness of your heart. Standing firm is having a fixed commitment to God and your faith in God. It is having a firm foundation in which going through the wilderness establishes in you. When we stand firm in our identity of God, we are proclaiming that our God never changes, He is immovable, and the promises He has spoken over our lives will come to pass on His timing.

Standing firm in our faith in God prevents us from burdening ourselves by the chains or yoke of slavery. For us to be rooted in our identity of God, we must not become burdened again by the yoke of slavery. For our identity is not in our brokenness that we must overcome, but it is in the God who healed, forgave, and redeemed our brokenness. It is not in the broken heart, pride, cracks, scars, and unforgiveness. That is not our identity; that is not what we are defined by. It's what the enemy wants us to be defined by because then we are still living in the chains of slavery. We are still living in our unworthiness, our identity crisis, and our brokenness. Yet, standing firm in our faith in God, knowing that Christ is our freedom gives us hope that the burden of becoming yoked by slavery will not manifest.

I find it interesting that Paul, the writer of Galatians, wrote that Christ set us free for freedom. Then he goes to write, almost as a reminder, that we must stand firm and not let ourselves become burdened again by the yoke of slavery. Paul is saying the remedy for not letting ourselves become burdened again is to stand firm in the freedom that Christ has set us free. He intentionally put these sentences together because he knew there is only one rescue from the yoke of slavery, Christ. Though this is the Good News, I think it's important that we understand what it means to be yoked of slavery.

To be yoked is to be in bondage of someone or something, and slavery refers to sin. Paul is saying we are not to be yoked or in bondage by the sin of our slavery. Remember in John 8:34 (NIV), Jesus says, "Very truly I tell you, everyone who sins is a slave to sin." Our sin, which is our unworthiness and lack of identity, is the cracks we keep open because we are comfortable, putting our identity in something or someone other than God. And the pride that keeps us from forgiving and fully healing is our master and bondage over our heart. In Lamentations, the prophet Jeremiah describes how his yoke of slavery affects him, "My sins have been bound into a yoke; by his hands they were woven together. They have been hung on my neck" (Lamentations 1:14, NIV).

Our sin becomes our slavery because we are allowing it to rule our lives. Do not let the yoke of slavery hang upon your neck, weighing you down with every step you take. Remember, Jesus has set us free from our yoke of slavery. The cracks of unworthiness and identity are not what break our hearts. Rather, those wounds can heal. It is when the cracks of unworthiness and identity prevent us from forgiving fully. When unworthiness and identity become the whole heart is when these cracks become the most broken part of the heart. That part becomes the yoke of our slavery. It becomes the sin of our hearts.

As we remember what Jesus did for us on the cross and that God is our identity, this yoke of slavery will not be the whole of our hearts. It will be the yoke of God that becomes us. His yoke is love, forgiveness, healing, protection, gentleness, and light. Our Lord Jesus says, "Come to me, all you who are weary and burdened, and I will give you rest. Take my yoke upon you and learn from me, for I am gentle and humble in heart, and you will find rest for your souls. For my yoke is easy and my burden is light" (Matthew 11:28–30, NIV). Take what Jesus says to heart. As you submit yourself wholly to Him, your yoke of slavery will be the yoke of Jesus. No longer will unworthiness plague the heart, and no longer will you be unidentified. Your cracks are a testament to the freedom that Jesus conquered for you.

Look at Luke 7:47 (NLT), "I tell you, her sins—and they are many—have been forgiven, so she has shown me much love. But a person who is forgiven little shows only little love." A little back story of this verse is that Jesus was invited to a Pharisee's house, and a woman who was well known to be sinful heard that Jesus was at this Pharisee's house. She went there and brought her perfume jar, which at this time was considered expensive to buy.

When she saw Him, she began to weep, and tears dropped on His feet. These very same tears she wiped off with her hair. When the Pharisee saw what the woman was doing, he showed disgust and looked at Jesus in bewilderment because He was allowing her to do that because of her sins. Simon, Jesus' disciple, also portrayed this same emotion, so Jesus told Simon, "Do you see this woman? I came into your house. You did not give me any water for my feet, but she wet my feet with her tears and wiped them with her hair. You did not give me a kiss, but this woman, from the time I entered, has not stopped kissing my feet" (Luke 7:44–45, NIV). This woman gave Jesus all she had so that she would be forgiven of her sins, but the most important part is she did it out of faith and love. She understood that Jesus was her loving, forgiving King, while the others had a heart of pride, disgust, and an air of loftiness.

As I said at the beginning of this chapter, unworthiness and our identity cannot be healed on our forgiveness. Only by God's forgiveness can we be healed. Once God has healed those cracks, forgiveness is fuller in our hearts. We can give out that forgiveness to others, to God, and to ourselves. In return, we can receive that forgiveness from God or from the ones who hurt us. Listen, God already knows that we have sinned, especially harboring the sin of unworthiness and lack of identity, yet, He still forgives because of what His Son did and God's desire for a relationship with His children. What this verse shows to us is that when we come to God with a heart that wants to be forgiven, that wants to be healed, He will be our Savior. He will be our Savior because our love for Him is more than our brokenness.

Our love for Him is like His love for us. We were created by Him; thus, we have His same love in our hearts. The Apostle Paul wrote,

Love is patient, love is kind. It does not envy, it does not boast, it is not proud. It does not dishonor others, it is not self-seeking, it is not easily angered, it keeps no record of wrongs. Love does not delight in evil but rejoices with the truth. It always protects, always trusts, always hopes, always perseveres. Love never fails.

1 Corinthians 13:4–8 (NIV)

This love is the truth—the truth of our forgiveness and the truth of His forgiveness. The truth is that love conquers brokenness, and the truth is love is worthy. When God shows us this love, we, in turn, show Him love, and just as importantly, we show others love. Even people who have hurt us. When we show the people who have hurt us our love, then we will be forgiven much, but if we show little love, then we will be forgiven little.

Only when we show God's love first will we be able to forgive others. The first and greatest commandment Jesus gave us is, "Love the Lord your God with all your heart and with all your soul and with all your mind" (Matthew 22:37, NIV). God comes first, above anyone, even above yourself. When we put Him first, then the love of God will overwhelm our cracked hearts into healing and forgiveness, enabling us to love others in return. This leads to Jesus' second commandment, "Love your neighbor as yourself" (Matthew 22:39, NIV). Even when others do not love you still, you must love them as Jesus would. If you do not, then your heart cannot forgive, and your heart will not heal. Let the love of God consume you.

In Psalm 63:3–4 (NIV), the psalmist sings about God's love proclaiming, "Because your love is better than life, my lips will glorify you. I will praise you as long as I live, and in your name I will lift up my hands." When God's love consumes us, we have no choice but to worship Him. We worship Him because of His worthiness in us, His identity that is our makeup, and His forgiveness in us that we give freely to others. Worshiping God is submitting ourselves wholly to Him. That means submitting our broken hearts, scars, cracks, and all. We are choosing Him above all else. So, we worship because God is "worthy, our Lord and God, to receive glory and honor and power, for you created all things, and by your will they were created and have their being" (Revelation 4:11, NIV). Worship Him knowing that your cracks are filled with His worthiness, His identity, and His love; that will turn your heart from being scarred to cracked to being filled.

CHAPTER 8

Filled

"Be kind and compassionate to one another, forgiving each other, just as in Christ God forgave you" (Ephesians 4:32, NIV).

Hearts are meant to beat with the goodness of life. They are not meant to drown in the dark, bitterness, hate, and anger that brokenness brings. They are not meant to be scarred or cracked for the rest of our lives. Hearts were created by God, designed by God, and are for God. Our hearts are meant to be filled by the everlasting God. This is accomplished only when we get to the last stage of forgiveness: forgiving the ones who have hurt us. Our hearts started the first healing process of becoming scarred, then overcame the two cracks (unworthiness and lack of identity) that only God could heal. This leads to the next stage of our healing process, that is, our hearts being filled with the love of God.

As I was going through my forgiveness process, this part of the stage was difficult for me. I had let my heart become scarred, no longer wanting to be the broken person that I was. After a few years of my scarring, I moved onto the next stage, my heart's cracks. I struggled to overcome the unworthiness that I felt and to discover where my identity lay. I battled with the constant negative words and emotions of unworthiness. The enemy would whisper into my ear that I wasn't good enough for God or that I was a terrible person and daughter. I would constantly push my talents and abilities to the side because I wasn't worthy of them. But mostly, I thought I was unworthy to receive God's love, forgiveness, and healing. I questioned Him on why He would ever choose me because of the sins I have committed and the broken heart I harbored.

Because I lost my sense of worthiness, I also lost my identity. I didn't know who I was in God. I labeled myself horrible things, or I put my identity into the things of this world. I struggled but was determined to overcome. There were plenty of tears and prayers in discovering that my worthiness lies in God, that my identity is in God. Yes, this stage was a growing stage for me, and still, I sometimes have to remember that I am worthy of God and my identity is in Him. After I overcame this stage, I moved on to the next: filled forgiveness.

The next stage, filled forgiveness, is about forgiving the ones who have hurt you. So, when God brought this to my attention, my initial reaction was, "God, how can You make me do this? How can I forgive him more? Hasn't he taken enough from me? Now, You want me to give him my love and total forgiveness. I don't know if I can. I don't know if I have any more strength left in me." Boy, was I ever wrong to question God. He knows what He's doing. He taught me a lesson during this stage. We will never move on from our broken hearts if we do not love our enemies as He loves them. We cannot be the judge of them. We must love everyone the way Jesus loves us. If we allow unforgiveness to settle in our hearts, then we will not amount to the glory that God created us to be.

With that, I want to turn to our scripture, "Be kind and compassionate to one another, forgiving each other, just as in Christ God forgave you" (Ephesians 4:32, NIV). In this verse, the first statement that is made is to be kind. When we forgive others, we cannot forgive with a sarcastic heart, a bitter or hateful heart, or an apathetic heart. We must first be kind to the people who have hurt us. I think this is one of the hardest things to do because our immediate reaction is to reject this idea of being kind to people who have hurt us. Our initial reaction is to defend ourselves and avenge our broken hearts. But isn't God our defender and judge? We cannot let pride take hold or offense settle in our hearts. Jesus did not let it when you sinned and broke His heart. He showed you kindness by dying on the cross so that you were saved for eternity. Shouldn't you do the same thing He did for you, or does your selfishness take over? The prophet Micah tells us what God requires of us, "[T]his is what he requires of you: to do what is right, to love mercy, and to walk humbly with your God" (Micah 6:8, NLT).

Kindness is in everyone because God is kindness. Remember He created you. If God is kindness, then you are kindness. Even a broken heart possesses kindness, but a heart that is being filled by God has all His kindness. Kindness is a characteristic of Him, "But when the kindness and love of God our Savior appeared, he saved us..." (Titus 3:4–5, NIV). Let go of unforgiveness and show kindness like Jesus. I know the people that hurt you are your enemies, but show them love because you were once an enemy of Jesus. I think Jesus said it best,

> But to you who are listening I say: Love your enemies, do good to those who hate you, bless those who curse you, pray for those who mistreat you. If someone slaps you on one cheek, turn to them the other also. If someone takes your coat, do not withhold your shirt from them. Give to everyone who asks you, and if anyone takes what belongs

to you, do not demand it back. Do to others as you would have them do to you.

If you love those who love you, what credit is that to you? Even sinners love those who love them. And if you do good to those who are good to you, what credit is that to you? Even sinners do that. And if you lend to those from whom you expect repayment, what credit it is that to you? Even sinners lend to sinners, expecting to be repaid in full. But love your enemies, do good to them, and lend to them without expecting to get anything back. Then your reward will be great, and you will be children of the Most High, because he is kind to the ungrateful and wicked. Be merciful, just as your Father is merciful.

Luke 6:27–36 (NIV)

Your enemies are not your enemies. Your enemies are your greatest kindness. God did not put them in your path so you could fight a gruesome and bloody war. No, He put them in your path to turn your heart from broken and hurt to filled kindness, a kindness that builds your enemies up, that loves your enemies through all the insults they hurl and encourages that in your brokenness, there is hope for a filled, complete heart of forgiveness. To fully forgive is to fully bless those who have hurt you. Put kindness into action with the truth of God. God doesn't want our hearts to become bogged down by our brokenness. He wants us to give the same love He gives us daily, a love that collides with kindness.

This love is light. A light that we share with our enemies. Our enemies are bathed in darkness, but God has put them in our paths so we can be the light that they need. When we were living in darkness, who revived us? Who scattered the shadows? Despite our failings, God still chose us to put His light in our hearts. He was and is still faithful. "I have loved you with an everlasting love; I have drawn you with unfailing kindness" (Jeremiah 31:3, NIV). We need, also, to give our love, our light, to others who need it the most. Even when we are still hurting, we must give, for the hurting will cease when our unforgiveness of others turns into loving, kind forgiveness.

The love we give to others is a love that will bring our hearts wholly together. When love is at the root of our forgiveness, then we will surely bear fruit. We will become fruitful in all we do. "But the fruit of the Spirit is love, joy, peace, forbearance, kindness, goodness, faithfulness, gentleness and self-control" (Galatians 5:22–23, NIV).

If bitterness, anger, hate, and pride are the root of forgiveness, then the heart will still be broken. We have not truly forgiven our enemies. We are still looking at our enemies from the world's viewpoint. We see them as a chance to avenge ourselves and to judge them by our standards, not God's. We are rejecting the very thing that can heal us fully: kindness, love, and God's forgiveness. Choose wisely which course you want to take. One will bear fruit, and the other will be rotten.

Seeking the truth of God in our kindness brings us His everlasting love. This love and kindness entangle our hearts, in which "the darkness is passing and the true light is already shining" (1 John 2:8, NIV). Dear one, letting go of your unforgiveness brings the flood of His light within you, letting it shine forth so others can see you are pure, holy, forgiven, healed, and loved by God.

Kindness and love are essential, but for them to have meaning, there needs to be compassion. Compassion is our next statement in our scripture, "Be kind and compassionate to one another…" We cannot have kindness and love if we do not have compassion in our hearts. All are closely tied to one another, in which compassion is the bond that brings them together. Without compassion, there is no mercy, for mercy is compassion. This is the same mercy that God showed us when Jesus was sacrificed. If we show no compassion, then we cannot possibly show kindness and love. We would not be able to forgive and allow our hearts to be filled and fully healed. We would ultimately be the unmerciful servant. One of Jesus' parables was that of an apathetic servant.

It goes like this: there was a great king that wanted to settle the debt of his servants. The first servant came. The king declared that this servant owed him ten thousand bags of gold. However, there was no way this servant could pay him all of that, so the king ordered the servant, his wife, and children to be sold to repay this debt. In a final desperate cry for help, the servant flung himself at the king's feet and pleaded to the king that he would pay everything back in due time. The king saw the desperation and angst on the servant's face, so he showed compassion and canceled the debt, letting the servant go.

This servant left the king's palace with a lighter heart and a skip to his step. He felt as if he had just won a great war and that he was the savior of mankind. As he was rejoicing with himself, he saw a fellow servant who owed him a debt of a hundred silver coins. However, this servant could not pay the debt. The other man grabbed him and began to choke him, demanding that he pay back the debt. The fellow servant started begging him to be patient and that he will find a way. But the man would have none of it; instead of showing compassion, the same compassion that was shown to him, the man threw the fellow servant into prison until he could pay back the debt.

Meanwhile, the scene that was unfolding was being watched by other servants. As they watched, they became angry and went to the king to report it. The king called in the man who owed ten thousand bags of gold and called him wicked because he had shown him compassion, but the man could not show the same compassion on his fellow servant. The king then threw this man into prison until he could repay all his debt.

At the end of Jesus' parable, He went on to say, "This is how my heavenly Father will treat each of you unless you forgive your brother or sister from your heart" (Matthew 18:35, NIV). When you have compassion for those who have hurt you, it becomes easier to forgive because kindness and love are present. Jesus, Himself, understood this, which is why He gave us this parable. We cannot become the unmerciful servant. If we do, then we will not be going to God's kingdom. With His great compassion, "He has given us new birth into living hope through the resurrection of Jesus Christ from the dead, and into an inheritance that can never perish, spoil or fade" (1 Peter 1:3–4, NIV). The kingdom is our inheritance.

God has given us a heart of compassion for the strong and the weak and for those who have hurt us. Think of how many times we have hurt God. How many times have you sinned against God, disobeyed? Turned your back on Him? Be honest with yourself. Now, how many times has God shown you kindness, love, forgiveness, and compassion? Every time you hurt Him, how many times did He show compassion? When I think of all the times I hurt Him, and I think of the times He showed me kindness, love, forgiveness, and compassion, the latter far outweighed the former. This is the same way we must show compassion. Paul wrote to the Corinthians, "Praise be to the God and Father of our Lord Jesus

Christ, the Father of compassion and the God of all comfort, who comforts us in all our troubles, so that we can comfort those in any trouble with the comfort we ourselves receive from God" (2 Corinthians 1:3–4, NIV).

Our hearts must be filled with kindness, love, and compassion. Bitterness, anger, hate, pride, and selfishness are perilous to carry around. When kindness, love, and compassion fill our hearts, then we will be able to forgive others, "just as in Christ God forgave you" (Ephesians 4:32, NIV). Our hearts will be healed fully in forgiveness.

SECTION 4

HEALING

CHAPTER 9

Open Heart

"Now devote your heart and soul to seeking the LORD your God"
(1 Chronicles 22:19, NIV).

An open heart. What does that mean? Well, if we look at its opposite, a closed heart, we connotate this as being closed off from people and emotions. A closed heart is a stubborn heart, one that wishes not to be healed from past or present hurts, one that wishes to be lonely in despair, one that is cold and distant. That probes the question, what is an open heart? An open heart is a heart that is now filled with kindness, love, compassion, and forgiveness that has settled in all the cracks. An open heart is a heart that is ready to receive complete healing. It's a heart that cannot allow for just forgiveness to be present; rather, it allows for renewal with healing. It becomes the very thing that God designed it to be, a heart that is only for Him.

At the very beginning of this book, in the first chapter, I talked about our hearts. I talked about how if we are not careful in the course of our actions, then what we choose becomes more heartbreak and brokenness. That choice, in regard to our hearts, is essential to God. We have reached a pinnacle point with our hearts. No longer are our hearts devoted to our brokenness that once became our identity, but our hearts are devoted to God. Our hearts are desperately seeking God for His complete healing.

We no longer want to just have kindness, love, compassion, and forgiveness in our hearts. We want something more. We want the whole of God. The completeness of God.

Our hearts are the center of our life. They are the whole of us. The vital function that makes us stay alive. Each heart is unique to the person it belongs to. From the heart come our emotions and desires. That is why it's so important that our hearts are not broken to the point of no return. We must take care of our hearts physically as well as spiritually. When we think of our hearts as being the center of our life, we think of it from a physical viewpoint. The heart pumps oxygen and blood throughout our bodies to sustain life. Actually, according to WebMD, the heart "beats 100,000 times per day, pumping five or six quarts of blood each minute, or about 2,000 gallons per day."[12] While this is astounding, we must not think of the heart as just purely physical. We must think of the heart from a spiritual viewpoint that is just as important as the physical viewpoint.

The spiritual aspect of the heart is our inner man, our innermost being. This brings into focus our healing hearts. Our healing hearts determine the course of our action. The action of what we do. Do we harbor hate, unforgiveness, pride, bitterness, or turn our hearts to forgiveness, worthiness, kindness, compassion, and healing, knowing that "everything you do flows from it" (Proverbs 4:23, NIV)? When our inner man is broken, separated from God, then our healing cannot take place. We are still uncircumcised; that is, we are still attached to our brokenness. An uncircumcised heart is a heart that is not bound to God. But that doesn't mean God abandons us there. No, He wants us to heal our hearts completely so that we can be the whole of Him. He gives us a way for this healing, His Word. "The word is very near you; it is in your mouth and in your heart so you may obey it" (Deuteronomy 30:14, NIV). Moses said these words because He knew that God's Word is the way to circumcise our hearts from our brokenness. This is why the psalmist says in Psalm 51:10 (NIV), "Create in me a pure heart, O God."

When God circumcises our hearts, a change occurs. A change from brokenness to healing takes place: a transformation, a renewal. Let me take you to Ezekiel. Ezekiel was a prophet, and God had given him multiple visions of Israel's destruction and restoration. One of the visions that I am going to describe to you is of Israel's restoration, more accurately, Israel's restored heart.

The vision starts by God telling Ezekiel that though His chosen people are scattered in many countries, He will eventually bring them back to their land, Israel. Once His chosen return, they must remove anything that is an idol. And for those who have obeyed God with their hearts, He will renew their hearts, turning them from a stony heart to a renewed and holy heart. This is how Scripture describes it, "I will give them an undivided heart and put a new spirit in them; I will remove from them their heart of stone and give them a heart of flesh. Then they will follow my decrees and be careful to keep my laws. They will be my people, and I will be their God" (Ezekiel 11:19–20, NIV).

Our hearts go through this same renewal, but we must first remove our idols, our sins, and our brokenness. We cannot see ourselves as unworthy or having no identity. We cannot be prideful, angry, hateful, or bitter during our healing process of brokenness. If we become any of this and can't let go of our hindrances, then there will be no renewal of the heart. And with the heart, it is critical not to hold onto hindrances. A heart that is still broken will not be a heart that believes in God and the righteous in God. It will not be a renewed heart.

Keeping our hearts open solely to God's love, kindness, compassion, and forgiveness becomes a dwelling place of God. We can see this firsthand when the Apostle Paul tells us that the Holy Spirit is "in our hearts as a deposit" (2 Corinthians 1:22, NIV). When your heart is broken, do you ever feel this yearning of being set free? Of cutting off the chains of bitterness, anger, hate, pride, and despair? And if you do become angry, bitter, hateful, or prideful, do you feel this sense of dread and guilt? A sense that your heart is divided? Well, if you feel any of that or somewhere in your heart you feel a squeeze, then that is the Holy Spirit convicting you. That's the Holy Spirit letting you know that it's not God's way. This is the Holy Spirit that indwells in you, in us.

Another example of the Holy Spirit dwelling in our hearts is found in the Book of Romans, "God's love has been poured out into our hearts through the Holy Spirit, who has been given to us" (Romans 5:5, NIV). Essentially, because the Holy Spirit dwells in our hearts, so do God and Jesus because they are all one and the same. Therefore, we must take care of our hearts and be open to the healing of God. We must not clog our hearts up with brokenness. It's not healthy. Devote your hearts wholly to God.

Our devotion to God goes beyond our hearts. It goes to the devotion of our souls. Understand this, our hearts and souls are connected, but we cannot have a heart if we first don't have a soul. Our souls are the essence of life. Our souls are filled with God's breath, breathing life into us (see Genesis 2:7). Our souls are holy in and of themselves. However, they can be broken just like the heart. The enemy goes for the soul because it lives for eternity, unlike the heart. What we put in our souls determines the outcome of our eternal standing. To put it more bluntly, our souls will either go to heaven or hell. When we continue to stay broken, our souls grieve because it's not right with God. We are designed to be completely whole and holy in God. Our souls long to be with God; it calls out with a longing that cannot be described. Scripture puts it like this, "As the deer pants for streams of water, so my soul pants for you, my God" (Psalm 42:1, NIV). Yes, our soul thirsts for God!

Like I said before, when our hearts aren't in the right standing with God, then our souls aren't either. So, when we are broken and swirling with negative emotions, then our souls grieve to be unchained. It is not the people that hurt us that our souls want us to avenge; rather, it's letting go of all the hurt, pain, brokenness, and unforgiveness that is the right way. We must understand that we cannot "be afraid of those who kill the body but cannot kill the soul. Rather, be afraid of the One who can destroy both soul and body in hell" (Matthew 10:28, NIV).

God taught me a valuable lesson in having an open heart and soul. When I was going through my healing process, a negative coping mechanism was revealed to me. I mentioned this at the beginning of the book, but I want to touch more on it. The negative coping mechanism that I developed when I was with my father was every time he would yell at me or become somewhat physical, I would shut down completely. I would shut down my mind and heart. I forced myself not to show or feel any emotion. If I did show emotion, then my father would pounce on that, and the situation would become worse. In my mind, showing and feeling no emotion was better than getting hurt, resulting in more brokenness. Because of this negative coping mechanism that I developed, another one became prominent. When something happened to me, I wouldn't go to anybody for help. I wouldn't talk about my feelings, and I wouldn't describe how everything made me feel.

Honestly, it was devastating to my heart and soul. I wasn't only hurting myself, but I was hurting my loved ones as well. I would push them away when they tried to help, shut down completely, or become angry. I was ruining the relationships that I most loved and needed. It wasn't just loved ones that I pushed away; I also pushed God away. The one relationship that I needed the most. My heart was becoming more and more closed off every single day.

Then one day, I had a vision. In my vision, I was in the middle of the ocean and struggling to swim. No, that's not being honest. I was drowning. I was completely submerged in the water, and occasionally if I kicked hard enough, my head would break the surface but only for a second before I was swept underneath again. I was desperately trying to swim to the surface but felt an incredible force pulling me further under. I remember it feeling so real. I remember the taste of the salt as I swallowed water; I remember feeling something on my ankle pulling me to the depths of the water, and I remember looking up, desperately searching for something. I could feel my legs, arms, and lungs burning from the exertion of keeping my body up. And I remember the overwhelming feeling of being exhausted and the fight leaving my body. I remember it all like it just happened yesterday.

In my desperation to reach the surface and my franticness of searching, I saw Him. I saw Jesus at the surface. I told myself, "I have to get to Him. He's my only help. My only Savior in this abyss." So, I called for Him. No answer, no movement to rescue me. I called for Him again. And again, nothing. At this point, I was ready to give everything up, but then He called my name.

He said, "Kaela, let go."

I answered back, "I can't. I don't know how."

He said, "Yes, you do, My daughter. Who is the holder of your heart and soul? Who fills your heart with love and hope? Who holds your heart in protection? Who has already forgiven you for all your sins?"

I replied, "You do, Lord. You do. But I am so fearful of my heart getting hurt again. I am so fearful that once I let go, I will become more broken than I already was."

Jesus said, "No, My child. Your heart is what makes you beautiful, even when it's broken. I am your Healer and protector. Letting go means giving Me all of the control, giving Me all of your heart, and giving Me all of your soul. I am your Creator, and I have created you to live in harmony with me as My daughter. For I am your true Father."

With that answer, I finally understood. He was bigger than my fears, bigger than my brokenness, and bigger than my faults. He was my Father who loves unconditionally, protects with fierceness, and never fails. When Jesus reached down into the water, I chose to grab His hand. He pulled me to the top, and I was standing on the water, letting go of my heart and soul to Him. No longer did I want to drown, but I wanted to be open and filled with Him. If I had chosen to stay in control of my heart and soul, letting fear be my factor, then I can assure you I wouldn't be here right now writing this.

The way we handle our brokenness determines the state of our souls. This is why I urge you to open your heart and soul to the renewal and complete healing of God. Don't become a blackened heart and soul. Become the light for others who are also broken. I urge you to seek God with your whole being. Don't become the wasteland that the enemy wants you to become. Rather, become the radiant, full of love and kind person that God created you to be. He brought you through this brokenness so that you would have a testimony to share with others who are going through the same thing. He brought you through this to give you a heart that is always open to Him.

CHAPTER 10

Faith in Healing

"Now faith is confidence in what we hope for and assurance about what we do not see" (Hebrews 11:1, NIV).

As we come and go through the process of opening our hearts to God, we encounter something eternal, something marvelous. We encounter faith, having a relentless faith in our healing. This is so important because if we don't have faith in our healing, then we will not have a fully open heart with God. We will not have a fully healed heart. We must believe. We must have the ultimate faith that God is our Healer.

To have faith in our healing, we first need to look at the beginning. We need to understand how powerful faith is and what faith is. Having faith in God is first having faith in the beginning. What I mean is having faith that God is the Creator of all things. He is the Creator of this earth, the land, the sea, the animals, and us. He formed everything, and we came from the dust of the earth that He molded to His great perfection. We must have faith that God is real, that there is no one or nothing else but God. If you cannot simply believe that God is your Creator and the Creator of all things, then you cannot possibly believe in all other things. You must first choose to believe in the simple before you can believe in the impossible.

After believing that God is the Creator of all, then we must have an understanding of what faith is. Faith is trust; trust is faith. Once we believe this understanding of faith, it brings us to the establishment of our relationship with God. A trustworthy and faithful relationship. It's important to establish a trustworthy relationship with God for faith in our healing to take place. Understand, God is always faithful and always trustworthy. It is us who need to form and constantly build a trustworthy and faithful relationship with Him. This relationship is established through prayer, sanctification, and our actions. Let's take a closer look at these.

Prayer brings us intimately close to God. It's where we lay down all our problems and all our complications. But it's also where God heals us, redeems us, loves us, forgives us, and protects us. Prayer is where we get right with God. It's where we become one with Him. We have to initiate prayer. God will not force us to pray. In Scripture, it says, "Come near to God and he will come near to you" (James 4:8, NIV). We must choose and draw close to God in our prayer. It's a commitment we must make every single day. There can be no "off days" because the second we do is the second our flesh takes over. It's the second the enemy swoops in to "steal and kill and destroy" (John 10:10, NIV). Prayer is a necessity; it's a need, not a want. Establish your relationship with God through the edification of prayer.

We establish a relationship with God through sanctification, where we become more like Jesus every day. That means constantly purifying our hearts and souls through repentance and prayer. Being sanctified is the establishment of our faith in Him. It is having faith in Jesus that sanctifies us. Scripture says, "So in Christ Jesus you are all children of God through faith, for all of you who were baptized into Christ have clothed yourselves with Christ" (Galatians 3:26–27, NIV). So, when we clothe ourselves with Jesus and are baptized, not by Jesus but *into* Jesus, then we become more sanctified each day, edging towards faith in our healing.

The last way of establishing a relationship that is closely tied to sanctification is our actions. What we do in our daily lives and how we do it can have a positive or negative effect on our relationship with God. Remember the ripple effect? That everything you do or say affects the present and future? Well, that applies to our relationship with God.

Let's look at brokenness for an example. If we remain broken, hateful, angry, prideful, and blameful, then our relationship with God will become stilted, sometimes non-existent. Not because God is non-existent but because we have allowed the darkness of our sins to consume our hearts. A ripple effect will take a course in our lives, the lives around us, and our relationship with God. Our faith will start to fizzle out because of the darkness we have allowed to be stored up in our hearts. If we choose to let go of the brokenness, the hate, the anger, the pride, and the blame and choose forgiveness, love, kindness, compassion, and healing, then our relationship with God will grow. The ripple effect will be one of light in our lives, the lives around us, and our relationship with God. Our actions are important to our faith in God. It is through our actions that we can see faith in God. When we choose to pray and choose to sanctify ourselves, then our actions are for God. Our actions must be for God's will, not ours.

Forming a healthy relationship with God is important to having faith in God. When faithfulness is established in the relationship, then we are saying that God is the only one we can solely rely on, that He is most trustworthy. Faith is "an unshakable belief that God will do everything he has promised to do even before there is visible evidence to that effect."[13] Having that strong, unbreakable relationship with God shows us that "we live by faith, not by sight" (2 Corinthians 5:7, NIV). Think of it this way, let's look at it from the disciple's point of view. Every day the disciples walked with Jesus, saw Him perform countless miracles, and predict future occurrences that came true. They believed because they saw.

Before Jesus' time to be crucified came, He first told the disciples what would happen at the crucifixion and after the crucifixion, but they didn't believe Him. Yet, all that Jesus told came to pass. The disciples didn't have faith that He would rise again from the grave three days later. After His glorious resurrection, we read in the Bible that Jesus greeted the disciples. In His greetings, they didn't recognize Him because they didn't have faith. It was only when Jesus "showed them his hands and side" (John 20:20, NIV) did they believe again. Only when they physically saw Him did they believe. Such low faith the disciples had. Even after seeing all the miracles Jesus performed, they still had low faith.

Jesus didn't greet all the disciples at once. There was one he hadn't greeted yet, and that was Thomas.

> Now Thomas (also known as Didymus), one of the Twelve, was not with the disciples when Jesus came. So the other disciples told him, "We have seen the Lord!" But he said to them, "Unless I see the nail marks in his hands and put my finger where the nails were, and put my hand into his side, I will not believe.
>
> John 20:24–25 (NIV)

Thomas declared that he wouldn't believe it if he couldn't see. Such blasphemy! He had no faith that Jesus rose again even though He told all of them that He would, such blasphemy indeed. The story doesn't stop there. Jesus visited all the disciples again. This time, He visited all of them, and He specifically came up to Thomas. This was the interaction between Jesus and Thomas,

> Then he said to Thomas, "Put your finger here; see my hands. Reach out your hand and put it into my side. Stop doubting and believe." Thomas said to him, "My Lord and my God!" Then Jesus told him, "Because you have seen me, you have believed; blessed are those who have not seen and yet have believed."
>
> John 20:27–29 (NIV)

During this interaction, Jesus said something prominent, "Because you have seen me, you have believed; blessed are those who have not seen and yet have believed." Those who have never seen Jesus and believe every word He has said are blessed. Believing is a blessing. Hebrews 11 is a great example of what the blessing of faith is.

Hebrews 11 is known as the Hall of Fame of Faith. This chapter specifically focuses on people through the Bible that had faith in God. These people include Abel, Noah, Abraham, Jacob, Isaac, Joseph, Moses, and many more. There were so many people throughout the Bible that demonstrated faith the writer could not name them all. I am telling you this because every one of these people was blessed by God because of their faith in Him. If Abraham didn't have faith, then his descendants wouldn't be numerous, and the promised land wouldn't have been possible. If Moses didn't have faith in God, then he wouldn't have been the leader that God wanted Him to be. You see, "Without faith it is impossible to please God, because anyone who comes to him must believe that he exists and that he rewards those who earnestly seek him" (Hebrews 11:6, NIV).

The story of Jesus and His disciples resonates with our hearts. For our hearts to be healed properly and fully, we must "live by faith, not by sight" (2 Corinthians 5:7, NIV). The disciples didn't live by faith because their hearts were closed off to Jesus. We cannot see with our earthly eyes, or our hearts will be closed off from healing. We must believe that our healing will come because of our faith in our God. Listen to my story of living by faith, not by sight.

It started my first year of college basketball. I have told you a little bit about my college experience and how my first two years were hard for me. However, I didn't tell you what happened in my last two years. In my freshman and sophomore years, I hardly played. I only played when the team was winning by a lot of points. As others would put it, I got garbage time. This put a toll on my heart. It broke my heart. The truth is I didn't play a lot because I let what affected me off the court affect me on the court. Those two years, I was still dealing with a broken heart from my experiences with my father. I let it bleed over into my basketball, the one thing I loved the most. And because of that, I was mentally and emotionally wrought. I didn't play basketball the way I knew how to play, and it showed on the court.

To say those two years were trying for me is an understatement. There were many days that I wanted to quit, and there were many days that I almost followed through with it. I remembered one day I thought to myself, *This is it; I'm quitting. Right now.* I walked the hallway to my coach's office door and stopped at his door. I raised my fist to knock but couldn't force myself to. I thought, *Could I go without basketball? I love it, and it's the one thing I'm passionate about. The one thing God had gifted me with. Is it His will for me to do this?* I ended up turning around and getting out of the gym as fast as possible so that I wouldn't make a grave mistake. There were many days and nights that I cried, not because I didn't get playing time, but because my heart was still broken, and I had let it affect me throughout the areas of my life. My brokenness was like poison. It was spreading throughout all the areas of my life, rotting everything in its path.

Even though I was mightily struggling, I made a promise to myself and God that I wouldn't quit, that I would see this through to the end. On top of that, I prayed countless times to God, asking Him if I was doing His will by sticking with basketball. And every time, God would answer to me, saying it was His will and His blessing. So, I decided to use my little playing time as motivation. I decided to put in the hard work and get in the gym as much as possible to become the best player I could be. The talent and gift that God blessed me with was shooting, so every single day, I would practice shooting hoops in the morning and the evening. I made sure that I made at least three hundred shots every morning and every evening. I did that for three years.

When I started putting in the hard work and still didn't see any playing time, I started to doubt myself, and I started to doubt God. I questioned Him, "Why should I put in all this hard work if I don't see any results? If I can't play? I'm tired of putting in the hard work and sacrificing countless hours for a game called basketball. I'm tired." At this moment, faith was all I had to go on. Because of the faith and motivation that God put in me, my dream came true.

My junior year started normal. Practice on my own, go to classes, practice with the team, and then practice on my own again. It was the same schedule as the last two years. The team was getting closer to our first regular-season game of the year. At one practice, I could see the way God was moving His pieces. A couple of the girls had gotten injured, nothing much, just a bop on the head. They had to go through concussion protocol, in which they couldn't practice or play for a couple of days. None of the girls had any serious injuries. Our team was down a few girls. This one day, I was standing on the sidelines watching the starting four go over something when I heard my name called. My coach looked me straight in the eyes and said I was starting. To say I was shocked is an understatement. I was overjoyed, nervous, and afraid. God had provided a way, and all the hard work was finally paying off.

In my junior and senior years, I started all the games, and along the way, God blessed me tremendously. He even blessed the team with a National Championship. During those two years, He blessed me so much that I can't name them all, but He also taught me valuable lessons along the way. The blessings wouldn't have come if there wasn't faith. During my four years of college, faith was at the center. If I didn't have faith, I noticed my world got a little bit darker. Yes, there were times my faith wavered, and there were times that I got knocked down, but faith was my foundation. It's God's foundation. With faith, God was able to accomplish things I didn't even think of. He was able to use me in mighty and powerful ways. And for that, I am very grateful for all my years in college. I am thankful that He even gave me a chance to play basketball, let alone start and win a National Championship. Words can't describe how thankful I am for Him. For how much He gets all the glory!

None of that would have happened if faith wasn't prevalent. The same goes for a broken heart. If faith is not at the center of your healing, then your heart won't be healed. Your faith doesn't have to be strong. No, even faith the size of a mustard seed can move a mountain (Matthew 17:20–21). When I say to put all your faith in God, you best do it because your heart will eventually become a wasteland, and all your progress of overcoming a prideful heart, hurt, bitterness, anger, hate, and unforgiveness will be for nothing.

Remember the story of the woman with the blood issue? The one with great faith? Let's start there. Jesus was on a boat coming to shore. When He came to shore, a man named Jairus, a synagogue leader, fell at Jesus' feet, begging Him to heal his dying daughter. Jesus went with this man, and as they were trekking back to Jarius' home, a large crowd started to form around Jesus. In this large crowd was a woman who had been bleeding for twelve years. This woman had suffered for twelve years. She suffered from shame, from doctors poking and prodding her, and financial hardship. The doctors tried to heal her, but her condition was only made worse by their ministrations. When the woman heard about Jesus and all He did, she knew she needed Him.

When she saw Jesus in the middle of the crowd, she came up behind Him and touched the small corner of His cloak. Scripture reveals it like this, "Because she thought, 'If I just touch his clothes, I will be healed'" (Mark 5:28, NIV). Her faith in Jesus was so powerful that when she touched the small corner of His cloak, she was immediately healed. Right away, Jesus knew someone had touched His cloak. "At once Jesus realized that power had gone out from him. He turned around in the crowd and asked, 'Who touched my clothes?' 'You see the people crowding against you,' his disciples answered, 'and yet you can ask, 'Who touched me?'" (Mark 5:30–31, NIV)? Again, we see that the disciples didn't have the necessary faith that the woman had.

But Jesus kept looking around to see who had done it. Then
the woman, knowing what had happened to her, came and
fell at his feet and, trembling with fear, told him the whole
truth. He said to her, "Daughter, your faith has healed you.
Go in peace and be freed from your suffering."

Mark 5:32–34 (NIV)

This woman had such great faith that just one touch of His cloak
healed her completely. For it was by faith that healed her, by faith
that sent her in peace, and by faith that freed her from suffering.

When our faith is so strong that just the touch of God brings
healing, then our hearts will receive it. We must be willing to have
that faith, and we must exercise that faith to the fullest. When our
faith is at its fullest, we understand what faith is in that moment.
It is our hope. Our defender. Our provider. Our forgiver. Our
love. Our mercy. Our grace. Our healing.

We looked at how faith is powerful and what faith is. We see
that without faith, there is no healing, but with faith, the impossible is made possible. I said earlier that faith is trust and that it's
significant to our relationship with God. Well, in our chapter
scripture, we see that faith is our confidence. It's not just our trust
in God, but it's our confidence in God. Merriam Webster's Dictionary defines confidence as "the quality or state of being certain."[14]
Confidence is being certain that God is who He says He is, it's
being certain that His promises will come to pass, and it's being
certain that our confidence is in the faith we have.

Confidence is trusting in God to the max, no matter what
the circumstance looks like. Faith is being taken to the next level
when confidence enters. When confidence enters faith, then our
healing becomes more powerful than it once was. Our hearts search
for this confidence because it yearns to be healed and to have a

purpose. You see, when we place our confidence in God, we are saying that God will never fail us, disappoint us, or abandon us. The prophet Jeremiah puts it best:

> But blessed is the one who trusts in the LORD, whose confidence is in him. They will be like a tree planted by the water that sends out its roots by the stream. It does not fear when heat comes; its leaves are always green. It has no worries in a year of drought and never fails to bear fruit.
>
> Jeremiah 17:7–8 (NIV)

In essence, our broken hearts are like tree roots. If the heart's roots are rotting, it's because it's getting the wrong nutrients. Those nutrients are hate, pride, anger, bitterness, selfishness, and unforgiveness. A rotting heart will fear other people, and it will believe that God will allow something bad to happen again. A rotting heart will worry every time someone gets close to them. That kind of heart will not and cannot produce fruit. Everything about it will rot, from the leaves to the fruit and the roots.

On the other hand, a broken heart that has confidence in God is a healthy tree. That heart will plant its root deep in the confidence of God, allowing Him to heal the heart fully. Those roots are receiving the right nutrients such as love, kindness, compassion, forgiveness, healing, and redemption. Even when a storm tries to knock this tree down, the roots are so implanted, so deep, that the tree will not be uprooted. It may bend to the storm, but it's so anchored to God that it will not break and shatter. This tree, this broken heart, has the utmost confidence in God. And because of that confidence in God, the heart's healing is tangible.

On the flip side, not having confidence in God is dire. Confidence can be placed in someone else or ourselves, which we can contribute to being prideful and selfish. We went into depth a couple of chapters ago about what pride and selfishness can do to a broken heart. But for a broken heart that is on the verge of full healing, pride and selfishness will set the healing process back. Jesus tells a parable of those who are confident in themselves. It goes like this: two men went up to the temple to pray. One was a Pharisee and the other a tax collector. Now, both had committed sins, and both needed to repent. But look closely at how the Pharisee prayed versus how the tax collector prayed.

> The Pharisee stood by himself and prayed: "God, I thank you that I am not like other people—robbers, evildoers, adulterers—or even like this tax collector. I fast twice a week and give a tenth of all I get." But the tax collector stood at a distance. He would not even look up to heaven, but beat his breast and said, "God, have mercy on me, a sinner."

Luke 18:11–13 (NIV)

The Pharisee thought himself better than a robber, evil person, adulterer, and even the tax collector. He thought his sin was less than all others. But the tax collector understood that no matter what, the sin is still a sin, and no status can eliminate that sin but God. Listen to what Jesus said at the end of this parable. "I tell you that this man, rather than the other, went home justified before God. For all those who exalt themselves will be humbled, and those who humble themselves will be exalted" (Luke 18:14, NIV).

When confidence is turned away from God, we tend to exalt ourselves rather than the merciful God. Not only that, but we are putting ourselves above God, which is a big no-no. You should not be an idol, and other people should not be your idol. There is only one God, and He has no rival or equal. Putting your confidence in an idol will produce nothing. Absolutely nothing. There will be no healing, no forgiveness, no love, no mercy nor grace, no protection, and no provision. In Psalm, the psalmist describes what an idol is,

> Why do the nations say, "Where is their God?" Our God is in heaven; he does whatever pleases him. But their idols are silver and gold, made by human hands. They have mouths, but cannot speak, eyes, but cannot see. They have ears, but cannot hear, noses, but cannot smell. They have hands, but cannot feel, feet, but cannot walk, nor can they utter a sound with their throats. Those who make them will be like them, and so will all who trust in them.
>
> Psalm 115:2–8 (NIV)

Exalting ourselves will only lead to our downfall. It will lead to more broken heartedness. We may think that our heart will heal on its own by our standards; in reality, we are wasting away precious time that belongs to the Lord. He is the only one who can heal our hearts fully, which is why our confidence rests in Him only. In Proverbs, the psalmist describes the ways of the Lord and our confidence in Him.

> For the LORD detests the perverse but takes the upright into his confidence. The LORD's curse is on the house of the wicked, but he blesses the home of the righteous. He mocks proud mockers but shows favor to the humble and oppressed. The wise inherit honor, but fools get only shame.
>
> Proverbs 3:32–35 (NIV)

Don't you think it's time for God's healing to take place, to put your confidence and faith in Him wholly? The broken heart yearns for that confidence and faith. It yearns for all of Him. More so, our hearts yearn for hope. A hope that faith and confidence produce. We see this here in our chapter scripture, "Now faith is confidence in what we hope for…" (Hebrews 11:1, NIV). We hope because we have the faith and the confidence to grasp that hope. This hope is the full healing of our hearts, healing that we couldn't get on our own. Healing that only God can accomplish.

Hope in God is "the confidence that what God has done for us in the past guarantees our participation in what God will do in the future."[15] Hope is an expectation for what is in the future. And for someone whose heart is broken, their expectation is a forgiven, healed, and redeemed heart. Hope is what the Apostle Paul wrote, "But hope that is seen is no hope at all. Who hopes for what they already have? But if we hope for what we do not yet have, we wait for it patiently" (Romans 8:24–25, NIV). Our hope is powerful. It brings a change about us. When hope is present, then our God is present. Our healing is more present; it's right on the cusp of changing our hearts forever. Without hope, there is no chance that God will heal us. Darkness more readily settles in because we have nothing to hope for, nothing to live for. This hope we have comes from the resurrection of Jesus Christ.

He is whom we place our hope in. In whom we are healed fully. He was sacrificed and tortured for us so we could relate to Him, and He relates to us. He shares in our sufferings, and our hope is firm because of that knowledge. With the confidence that we possess, we can face our broken heart with courage and hope that we will overcome it and be healed of it.

> Therefore, since we have been justified through faith, we have peace with God through our Lord Jesus Christ, through whom we have gained access by faith into this

grace in which we now stand. And we boast in the hope
of the glory of God. Not only so, but we also glory in our
sufferings, because we know that suffering produces perseverance; perseverance, character; and character, hope.

Romans 5:1–4 (NIV)

When hope is given, a new light is lit within. It starts as a cloud
of smoke, but as it's fanned more and more, that smoke turns into
a small flame. That small flame turns into a fire that blazes forth.
This fire lights a path casting out all shadows and turning the
darkness to light. Some say hope can be dangerous, even deadly,
but the Word says, "those who hope in the LORD will renew their
strength. They will soar on wings like eagles; they will run and not
grow weary, they will walk and not be faint" (Isaiah 40:31, NIV).
So, hope in the impossible, hope in forgiveness, hope in healing,
and hope in redemption. At last, hope for your broken heart.

SECTION 5

REDEMPTION

Chapter 11

Redeemed Heart

*"He provided for his people; he ordained his covenant forever—
holy and awesome is his name" (Psalm 111:9, NIV).*

We have finally reached our last section of this book: redemption. Our journey through this book has been long, starting with addressing the brokenness inside our hearts to acknowledging that our hearts are prideful, venturing towards forgiveness of God and from God to the heart healing in fullness. Lastly, we come to our last stop on this journey, conquering our broken hearts once and for all. We come towards redemption. We turn our broken hearts into redeemed hearts—the redeemed heart of God.

With tentative but assured steps, let's end our journey with Jesus. Look at the chapter scripture, "He provided redemption for his people; he ordained his covenant forever—holy and awesome is his name" (Psalm 111:9, NIV). The psalmist makes no qualms about who he's talking about, Jesus. Jesus is the one who went through the testing or proving for our redemption so that the covenant will last forever, proclaiming how holy and awesome the Lord is! This scripture can be broken down into three sections. The first section is "He provided redemption for his people..." I just mentioned that "He" is Jesus, but I want to turn our attention to "provided" and "redemption."

When we think of provided, we think of something we need. We see that to provide is something we need to be delivered for us or to us. When we read in our chapter scripture that Jesus "provided redemption for his people," we understand that He is delivering or supplying us redemption. But in order for Jesus to provide redemption for us, He must go through testing or proving. And in the same way that Jesus is tested or proved, we also must go through the testing or proving.

"Proved" is a verb. When something is being proved, it is to show that something is the truth. Sometimes testing and proving become interchangeable words, and it's important to know they mean the same thing: truth. God can test or prove us in our level of faith, our level of forgiveness, our spiritual level, and where our heart is in Him. Our proving comes from the trials that we go through, such as our broken hearts. We see this in Isaiah, "See, I have refined you, though not as silver; I have tested you in the furnace of affliction" (Isaiah 48:10, NIV). When we are tested, then our hearts become tested on whether they obey God or disobey God, whether our hearts are of this world or God's world. Though the testing may be difficult, at times unbearable, we must recognize that our testing does not compare to the testing of Jesus.

He went through the ultimate proving. He went through it because, by providing redemption, Jesus first had to prove our redemption for us by the cross. It wasn't just Him sacrificing Himself on the cross for us but what He went through before the cross. It's how relatable Jesus became to us before His crucifixion. I think it starts back to Jesus being tempted by Satan in the wilderness. He was tempted three times by Satan, and each time, Jesus put him in his place with the Word of God (see Matthew 4:1–11). This shows us that though Jesus was tempted, He did not commit sins because of the conviction of the Word of God and the Holy Spirit.

Another human aspect of Jesus was when He didn't want to take the cup of suffering. He didn't want to die. And why would He? He is fully human, after all. He had already been ridiculed and mocked; He knew that once He committed to the cup of suffering, there was no going back. He wanted to live, not to die. Yet, because He is Lord, He knew what that cup of suffering meant for us. Love. Out of love, He took the cup of suffering because He didn't want to see His people be broken anymore. He wanted them to be in unity with Him always.

One last human aspect of Jesus was when He was being tortured and mocked before He was crucified. When Jesus was going through that torment, He had the power to command everyone to stop. He had the power to prevent His torture and mockery, but instead, He chose to be human. He chose us. Though His torturing left His face and body beyond recognition when He finally succumbed to death on the cross then rose three days later, He paid the price for our redemption. He proved our redemption.

Jesus' proving is a testament that we can overcome our proving. Even when we become tempted, hurt, angry, bitter, prideful, unforgiving, our proving has already been overcome by Jesus rising from the dead. Our proving is our broken heart, and in this proving, our faith in Him becomes proven. Our faithful or lack of faithful heart becomes exposed. The Apostle Peter tells it like this,

> In all this you greatly rejoice, though now for a little while you may have had to suffer grief in all kinds of trials. These have come so that the proven genuineness of your faith—of greater worth than gold, which perishes even though re-

fined by fire—may result in praise, glory and honor when Jesus Christ is revealed.

1 Peter 1:6–7 (NIV)

Our brokenness is proved in our faith in Jesus. We must understand that our faith in Jesus must be proved to bring His redemption into our hearts.

There were moments during my journey of healing where my faith was proved by what I couldn't see. My broken heart didn't just bleed into my everyday life; it bled into what I loved the most at that time, basketball. When I was struggling to comprehend everything during my freshman and sophomore years in college, I began to question God. I questioned Him because of what I saw with my fleshly eyes.

I saw other girls being blessed when I knew they didn't put the hard work in. I saw myself being pushed to the sidelines with not a glance from anyone. I saw how some girls treated each other and were still being blessed. I saw all of this and questioned God, "Why can't I be blessed like that? Why am I being pushed to the side when I put in so much hard work? Why am I even here if I am just going to sit on the bench the whole time? What's my purpose here? Is it just for that? As a follower of You, why am I not being blessed when those who don't follow You are?" These questions and many more ran rampant through my head all day long. Somehow, I even equated them to my worth. Sure, I was given encouragement and messages from God about my purpose on that team, but I was too blinded by what I saw to look deeper. My faith was shaken to its core. Doubting if I was operating in the will of God, doubting the gifts He blessed me with, and worst of all, doubting God.

God had to work on my heart. He had to humble me and remind me that it isn't about myself but Him. It's about Him being glorified, not me. It's about Him being praised, not me. It's about Him being worshipped, not me. As I was humbled, my eyes began to see a new perspective, God's perspective. My doubting became less and less, and though my faith was still a bit shaken, God was still constant. As my faith grew in Him and His greater purpose for my life and the lives of others, my redemption grew nigh. He was proving my faith by what I couldn't see. At the time, I couldn't see that He was moving all the pieces so He would get all the glory. I couldn't see that He was moving in some of my teammate's hearts. I couldn't see that He was using me to further His greater purpose. I was so stuck on my purpose, my glory, that I couldn't even see God. He was teaching me that for some people seeing is believing, but for His people, believing is seeing.

When God proves someone's faith, just like He did with Jesus, redemption comes next. We know that when Jesus was crucified, and He took His last breath, that was the start of His redemption and our redemption. After His last breath, there was a long, dark three days, then the miraculous happened. He rose from the dead and walked out of His tomb. That empty tomb became our redemption. Because Jesus was crucified, His blood is our atonement. Because He rose from the dead, He ables us to be made new. Repenting sincerely and accepting Jesus fully in our hearts, His sacrificial blood is our renewal. That is our redemption; our heart is the heart of Jesus. Our hearts died on that cross and rose from the tomb, becoming redeemed hearts. He is the provider of our redemption by the proving of our hearts.

What exactly is redemption? We know who our redemption comes from, and we know how we become redeemed, but what is redemption? Look at this definition, "Redeem, Redemption, Redeemer is to pay a price in order to secure the release of something or someone. It connotes the idea of paying what is required in order to liberate from oppression, enslavement, or another type of binding obligation."[16] I think this definition hits it right on the head and describes exactly what Jesus did for us. It's important to notice that though our redemption operates under the new covenant, Jesus, God has been redeeming His people from the beginning. Our redemption is sealed by the blood of Christ, which makes Jesus' death and empty tomb so special. Yet, even without Jesus, God was redeeming His people because He loves them so much.

Look at the Book of Exodus. Throughout the whole book, God was redeeming His people from the Egyptians and even themselves. Scripture says, "But it was because the LORD loved you and kept the oath he swore to your ancestors that he brought you out with a mighty hand and redeemed you from the land of slavery, from the power of Pharaoh king of Egypt" (Deuteronomy 7:8, NIV). It was here that God became God the Redeemer. Let's look at more Scripture,

> I am LORD, and I will bring you out from under the yoke of the Egyptians. I will free you from being slaves to them, and I will redeem you with an outstretched arm and with mighty acts of judgment. I will take you as my own people, and I will be your God. Then you will know that I am the LORD your God, who brought you out from under the yoke of the Egyptians.
>
> Exodus 6:6–7 (NIV)

As you read these verses, doesn't your heart yearn to be redeemed? Is brokenness your Egypt? Do you feel enslaved by this brokenness? I assure you that just as God redeemed His people, He will redeem you as well. Your faith must be proved, and there must be a sacrifice for your heart to be redeemed.

Once your faith is proven, and you sacrifice your old ways—that is, your old way of thinking, your anger, hate, bitterness, pride, and unforgiveness—then your redemption is nigh. Let's focus on Jesus again since, for us, He is our source of redemption. Our redemption is present because of our sin. Our sins can be a multitude of things, such as lying or adultery, but in this case, our sins are hate, anger, bitterness, pride, and unforgiveness. Our sin is not our brokenness; rather, it is the symptoms that come with brokenness, the symptoms that take root in our hearts. If the symptoms never took root, then we would not need redemption.

This is why Jesus is so critical to our redemption because He paid that blood price so we could be liberated from our sin. The Apostle Paul says that Jesus "gave himself for us to redeem us from all wickedness and to purify for himself a people that are his very own, eager to do what is good" (Titus 2:14, NIV). A redeemed heart has its sight set only on Jesus. A redeemed heart is like Jesus. Full of love, kindness, compassion, forgiveness, and humility. Two verses that capture redemption are "For he has rescued us from the dominion of darkness and brought us into the kingdom of the Son he loves, in whom we have redemption, the forgiveness of sins" (Colossians 1:13–14, NIV). No longer is the heart broken from the darkness that surrounds us and the darkness in others, but it is redeemed by Jesus Christ and loved fully.

When the loving redemption of Jesus enters your heart, everything else ceases to exist. Your heart becomes connected to God in a way that is unexplainable, and you begin to see God in a new light. The heart becomes filled with overwhelming emotions that only God can put there. The Holy Spirit takes residence and brings a warmth that spreads throughout. No longer do you see from a dark and gray lens; instead, you see all the vibrant colors of life. Your heart beats with a purpose, God's purpose, to do His will and not yours. To be obedient to Him and serve only Him. Your heart is no longer broken. It is redeemed. This redeemed heart is an everlasting covenant between Jesus and you. He died on that cross to usher in the new covenant for you.

In our chapter scripture, "He proved redemption for his people; he ordained his covenant forever—holy and awesome is his name," we have covered "proved," "redemption," and "covenant." Now, I want to turn our focus to "holy" and "awesome." These words are key elements because we can't just take and not give. We can't take Jesus' redemption without giving Him all the glory. We must glorify God because He is holy and awesome. Our purpose is to glorify God in all we do and the things we don't do.

When we give our heart fully over to Him, and He redeems our hearts, then we have no other option but to glorify Him. If we don't glorify Him, then are our hearts even truly redeemed? Isn't the whole point of giving our hearts over to Him to heal us, redeem us, and transform us completely, acknowledging that His ways are higher than our ways? When we don't glorify Him, we are signaling that it was by our might that our heart is redeemed. Don't let your heart become prideful and broken again. Glorify Him for His redemption because He is holy and awesome!

Let's look at our chapter scripture again. The psalmist made it a point to put the words "holy" and "awesome" in the same sentence. The psalmist made a point to say it is His name, which is holy and awesome. Take a look at "holy." We find the word throughout the Bible describing who God is. This evidence is found everywhere, such as in Isaiah 6:3 (NIV), "Holy, holy, holy is the LORD Almighty; the whole earth is full of his glory." Perhaps, the most convincing evidence of God's holiness comes from the experience of others throughout the Bible. Let me remind you, God's holiness manifests itself when your redemption is present. When your heart is right with God, then you will see His holiness.

The prophet Isaiah experienced God's holiness as such. The story goes like this, Isaiah saw God on His throne in heaven along with His angels. Isaiah saw these angels praising God, proclaiming He was holy. Immediately, when Isaiah saw the Lord, he cried out, "I am ruined! For I am a man of unclean lips, and I live among a people of unclean lips, and my eyes have seen the King, the LORD Almighty" (Isaiah 6:5, NIV). Isaiah's cry was one out of recognition. Recognition that he was a sinner and knowing his sin would defile God's throne. Not only that, but God was commissioning him to be a prophet, and Isaiah thought that he could not be so because of his sin.

As heartbroken people, we often think this way when God is in our presence. We condemn ourselves to the point that it affects our worth, and we hide our faces from God. We don't want Him to see all of our failures and all of our faults. Instead of being redeemed, we cower deeper into our broken hearts, refusing to let God heal and redeem. God can see everything, even the things we think we can hide.

Yet, let's continue with Isaiah's story. When God saw and heard Isaiah's struggle with his sin, He commanded an angel to cleanse him. The angel came to Isaiah holding a live, burning coal in his hand that the angel had taken from the Lord's altar. With that sacred and holy coal, the angel touched Isaiah's lips. This is what the angel said, "See, this has touched your lips; your guilt is taken away and your sin atoned for" (Isaiah 6:7, NIV). Instantaneously, Isaiah's sin and guilt were taken away. The result of being cleansed was this, "Then I heard the voice of the Lord saying, 'Whom shall I send? And who will go for us?' And I said, 'Here I am. Send me!'" (Isaiah 6:8, NIV). Because Isaiah accepted the cleansing of the Lord, God commissioned him to be His prophet. He sent him on a mission for His great purpose. We can apply this to our situation. When we allow God to cleanse our hearts, then we are allowing Him to commission us. However, it is only through God's holiness that we are redeemed like Isaiah.

Another experience about God's holiness is from Peter's story. This is the story of when Peter was first called to be a disciple of Jesus. His name at the time was Simon Peter. One day Jesus was preaching to a group of people on the shores of the Sea of Galilee. At the water's edge, there were two boats, and the fishermen were washing their nets. Jesus saw this and got into one of the boats. The boat He got into was Simon's, and Jesus asked Simon to move the boat away from the edge of the shore. Jesus continued to preach. When He had finished, He told Simon to move the boat to deeper waters and let down the nets to catch fish. Simon probably looked at Jesus like He was crazy because they had fished all night and caught nothing. Nonetheless, Simon obeyed, and when he cast down his net, he caught so many fish that the net began to break.

When Simon saw the miracle that it was, he prostrated himself at Jesus' feet. Then, Simon said something interesting. Instead of praising Jesus, he said this, "Go away from me, Lord; I am a sinful man" (Luke 5:8, NIV)! In Simon's heart, he recognized that Jesus is Lord, and because Jesus is Lord, He is holy. Again, we see Simon act the same way as Isaiah did. Simon thought his sins were too much for Jesus. He thought he couldn't be in the presence of Jesus because of his sins. He thought he was unworthy. Jesus didn't see him that way. With love, Jesus said this, "Don't be afraid; from now on you will fish for people" (Luke 5:10, NIV). And to further this, Simon left everything, his livelihood, all the fish he caught, everything he had ever known, and followed Jesus.

When holiness is present in our redemption, like Simon's, our heart is in the palm of God's hands. His holiness is what cleanses us from our head to our toes. Our broken hearts cannot prevent the Lord from proclaiming His holiness over our lives. God has called you to be holy in Him because He is holy. "Be holy because I, the LORD your God, am holy" (Leviticus 19:2, NIV). Obey Him for the redemption of your heart. Out of love, He called us to be holy, and out of love, He sent His Son so that our holiness is made tangible. I leave you with these verses,

> For he chose us in him before the creation of the world to be holy and blameless in his sight. In love he predestined us for adoption to sonship through Jesus Christ, in accordance with his pleasure and will – to the praise of his glorious grace, which he has freely given us in the One he loves.
>
> Ephesians 1:4–6 (NIV)

In Psalm 111:9, the psalmist doesn't just proclaim God is holy, but the psalmist says God is awesome. Awesome is just another word for reverence of God, standing in awe of God. In essence, it's a form of worship that God has redeemed us with. Reverence is often described as fear. But not the kind of fear that shakes you in your boots and causes you to be paranoid. No, this fear is the fear of the Lord knowing that He is holy and awesome. In the Book of Exodus, we see this reverence after the Ten Commandments were read to the Israelites. After the reading, there was thunder and lightning and the sound of a trumpet being blown. Where the Ten Commandments were given to Moses, Mount Sinai, the Israelites saw the mountain smoke. So, when the Israelites saw all of this, they "trembled with fear" (Exodus 20:18, NIV). Then, this is what happened, "They stayed at a distance and said to Moses, "Speak to us yourself and we will listen. But do not have God speak to us or we will die" (Exodus 20:19, NIV).

The Israelites were so fearful of God that they didn't want Him to speak to them. I want to make a point and say this was a reverence kind of fear. It was a fear that God is the Almighty, and He can do anything and everything. He caused the thunder and lightning, and He caused the mountain to smoke. Their fear was of the mighty power that God has. Moses said to the people, "Do not be afraid. God has come to test you, so that the fear of God will be with you to keep you from sinning" (Exodus 20:20, NIV). God put this fear within His people to prevent them from turning against Him and sinning. Never did God hurt them, threaten them, or force them to fear Him. Instead, He let His people choose whether to fear and obey Him.

This same thing applies to us. We must choose to obey and fear Him. We will encounter many struggles and trials, but when we revere God, we will be holy and triumphant in Him. "But even if you should suffer for what is right, you are blessed. Do not fear their threats; do not be frightened. But in your hearts revere Christ as Lord. Always be prepared to give an answer to everyone who asks you to give the reason for the hope that you have" (1 Peter 3:14–15, NIV).

Revering God can be just as simple as looking back on what God did for you in the past to what He is doing now and what He will do in the future. It's recognizing the handprints of God. It's seeing with spiritual eyes that God was in every aspect of your life. God is all-powerful and all-knowing.

From my experiences, God could have taken the obstacles out of my path. He could have made things easier. He could have moved pieces around so that there wasn't so much hurt, pain, bitterness, hate, and anger. He could have done all of that. But He didn't. He chose not to. He chose not to take the obstacles out of my path, He chose not to make things easier, and He chose not to move the pieces. That doesn't mean He wasn't there in my experiences because He was. Throughout this book, I have given you my experiences where God was active and where He saved me. The point is I had to come to terms with God, not changing my circumstances to make it easier. I had to come to terms with that my father wasn't going to change, and God wasn't going to change him because I wanted Him to.

Coming to terms with all of that seemed insurmountable to me. I went through a season of confusion, sadness, and hurt. I became angry and hurt by God because I wanted Him to change everything that was happening. I often posed questions like, "Why can't You? You are all-powerful. Will You change my father? Lord, why are You turning Your back on me?" Yet, with a revelation, I can now look back and see that I don't want Him to ever change anything. He knows what He is doing. If God had changed one minute detail, then perhaps I wouldn't have surrendered my heart over to Him. Perhaps I wouldn't have been saved.

I went through all those experiences not so the outside could change, but it was so I could change from the inside. He taught me to be resilient and endure to the end. He taught me to be obedient only to Him and not rely on man. He softened a hardened heart so His Holy Spirit could flow. He taught me to follow His footsteps and not the shadows of the world. His grace and mercy were my saving line. His love extinguished all the darkness. His light illuminated my lifeless soul. My experiences led me through struggles, but in the end, my struggles became my strength. They became my redeeming love.

CHAPTER 12

A Forever Heart

"It is because of him that you are in Christ Jesus, who has become for us wisdom from God—that is, our righteousness, holiness, and redemption" (1 Corinthians 1:30, NIV).

As we come to the end of our journey, let us not just become redeemed but fully redeemed, fully redeemed into a forever heart. A redeemed heart must be proved or tested through the trials of life. The trials that God will prove our faith in Him. During these trials, our hearts must make a choice whether to choose God above the circumstances or not. Once the choice is made clear, and God is at the center, then our hearts go through the process of redemption, a redemption that comes only at the hand of God. Our redemption from a broken heart is the redemption of Jesus. Jesus is our forever heart.

His heart is our heart because we are made in the likeness of Him. Knowing that our redeemed heart rests in Jesus becomes our forever heart. I want us to delve into what our forever heart is and how our broken heart becomes our forever heart. For this, we must turn to our chapter scripture. I will say this again; our forever heart comes from Jesus. Look, the chapter scripture says, "It is *because* of him that you are *in* Christ Jesus…" (emphasis added). Because of Jesus, our hearts are forever in Christ Jesus.

Let me break it down for you. Jesus is fully human and fully divine, meaning through His mother, Mary, He became fully human, and through His Father, God, He became fully divine. Sometimes it becomes hard for us to comprehend how Jesus could be fully human. It's easier for our minds to accept that He is fully divine because He rose from the dead, and only someone who is fully divine can do that. If we look at the Scriptures closely, we can see that He was also fully human.

> Who, being in very nature God, did not consider equality with God something to be used to his own advantage; rather, he made himself nothing by taking the very nature of a servant, being made in human likeness.
>
> Philippians 2:6–7 (NIV)

> For this reason he had to be made like them, fully human in every way, in order that he might become a merciful and faithful high priest in service to God, and that he might make atonement for the sins of the people. Because he himself suffered when he was tempted, he is able to help those who are being tempted.
>
> Hebrews 2:17–18 (NIV)

Because Jesus is fully human, He understands the brokenness of the heart. He went through the same brokenness that we have gone through. Our situation might be different than Jesus', but the result was the same: brokenness. But Jesus is fully divine, and because of this, our heart is no longer broken but redeemed; it's a forever heart. An eternal heart.

When our heart was broken, we had no leader, no ruler. Our broken heart was led by ourselves. It was led by hurt, pain, anger, bitterness, pride, and selfishness. Once we laid down ourselves at the feet of Jesus and surrendered our selfish ways to Him, then our hearts started the process of forgiveness. After forgiveness was healing and now redemption, our redeemed hearts cannot be led by our ways or thoughts but must be led by His ways and thoughts. Our forever heart lies in the Shepherd's hands.

A forever heart knows who the ruler of their heart is. They know who changed the course of the heart, and the ruler knows the forever heart. The ruler knows His people. That ruler is none other than Jesus. He takes care of the forever heart and teaches them His ways. Jesus said in the Book of John, "I am the good shepherd; I know my sheep and my sheep know me—just as the Father knows me and I know the Father—and I lay down my life for the sheep" (John 10:14–15, NIV). Jesus is the leader of the pack. He knows every single detail about you, even the details that nobody else knows. Likewise, in our hearts, we know Jesus. We are drawn to Him because He is the light of our hearts. He is our Creator, our Father. "For the Lamb at the center of the throne will be their shepherd; he will lead them to springs of living water. And God will wipe away every tear from their eyes" (Revelation 7:17, NIV).

Because we are in Jesus, He is "who has become for us wisdom from God…" (1 Corinthians 1:30, NIV). This part of the verse is what ushers in the reality of our forever hearts. Our wisdom of things concerning the heart comes from Jesus. Now, not everyone finds this wisdom, and certainly not every Christian. Having wisdom is more than speaking wise. Having wisdom is listening, hearing, and obeying the Holy Spirit. It's the same Holy Spirit that spoke to Jesus and guided Him on His journey.

Our wisdom does not come from man; it comes from Jesus, who is the Word. In actuality, our wisdom comes from the Word. As we know, God is Jesus and Jesus is God. Jesus is fully divine, and His father was the Father. So, when we read the verses in the Book of John, we must understand that our wisdom comes from Jesus.

> In the beginning was the Word, and the Word was with God, and the Word was God. He was with God in the beginning. Through him all things were made; without him nothing was made that has been made…The Word became flesh and made his dwelling among us. We have seen his glory, the glory of the one and only Son, who came from the Father, full of grace and truth.
>
> John 1:1–3, 14 (NIV)

Our forever hearts are governed by this wisdom. We cannot possibly have a forever heart if we follow the passions of the world. We cannot possibly have a forever heart if we blatantly refuse to listen, hear, and obey the leading of the Holy Spirit. It's in this wisdom we achieve the process of total redemption when we become totally surrendered to the wisdom of Jesus.

As we become enveloped in Him and driven by His wisdom, this leads to "our righteousness, holiness, and redemption" (1 Corinthians 1:30, NIV) in God. As we can see, this is the last segment of our chapter scripture, and yes, being in Jesus and led by His wisdom leads to our righteousness, holiness, and redemption in God. A righteousness of the heart, holiness of the heart, and the redemption of the heart. All three of these, we will cover. Let's start with the righteousness of the heart.

For us to have a righteous heart, we must first understand where righteousness came from. Or, more accurately, whom righteousness came from. According to Merriam Webster's Dictionary, "righteousness" is defined as "acting in accord with divine or moral law" and "morally right or justifiable."[17] God is morally right, and He judges right. Righteousness is a characteristic of God (Romans 3:5). He is righteous because He is good. He is inherently good. There is no evil inside of Him, no sin in His heart, and no darkness in His soul. We see this in the words of Moses, "He is the Rock, his works are perfect, and all his ways are just. A faithful God who does no wrong, upright and just is he" (Deuteronomy 32:4, NIV). Because God is righteousness, we also are righteous because of Jesus's sacrifice.

To have a righteous heart, we must seek His righteousness, which is accomplished by having faith that Jesus died on the cross for us. This is backed up by the Word of God in the Book of Romans,

> God presented Christ as a sacrifice of atonement, through the shedding of his blood—to be received by faith. He did this to demonstrate his righteousness, because in his forbearance he had left the sins committed beforehand unpunished—he did it to demonstrate his righteousness at the present time, so as to be just and the one who justifies those who have faith in Jesus.
>
> Romans 3:25–26 (NIV)

Having faith that Jesus cleansed us of our sins is the key. We cannot have a righteous heart if we still harbor sin.

Believing in the cross is our righteousness. It's God's love for us, bringing us in righteousness with Him. He wants to share with us, so grab hold of the cross and never let go. Don't take Jesus for granted because He took your sin and laid it upon His shoulders to carry. The weight of your sin is too much to bear on your shoulders. God sent His Son. "God made him who had no sin to be sin for us, so that in him we might become the righteousness of God" (2 Corinthians 5:21, NIV). Once we have planted our faith firmly in Jesus, then our hearts can become righteous. But we must exercise our faith daily. It is not a one-time deal. Every day there will be new obstacles, small or big, and our faith in Jesus is what will keep us grounded in Him. This faith is what brings righteousness to the heart, establishing it forever.

Once the heart is established in righteousness, the next course is a holy heart. Technically speaking, you cannot establish a holy heart because every day, we are striving to be holy. It must be a choice. Every day we must choose to be holy. It's not set in stone because we are human. We are sinners. There is only one who was every holy, and that's Jesus, yet every day, we choose to be holy like Him. We must sanctify (another word for holy) ourselves. It's a relief knowing that God chose us first to be sanctified by the Holy Spirit. He chooses us every single day and every single time, no matter what. He chose us even before we were born. When the Apostle Paul was writing his letters to the Thessalonians, he told them that we are chosen first before God and sanctified before Him by the Holy Spirit. "God chose you as first fruits to be saved through the sanctifying work of the Spirit and through belief in the truth" (2 Thessalonians 2:13, NIV).

I would like to define what it means to be sanctified. "Sanctification is the practice of godliness in the life of a believer, and especially to the process by which a person who has been saved progresses toward the goal of becoming like God and Christ."[18] By the leading of the Holy Spirit, our hearts want to be like God, like Jesus. Our hearts want to be holy like Him. It's a hunger that starts the moment He chooses us above all others and all things—becoming God-like stems from being created in His image. It stems from the moment Adam and Eve were created. They were born to live in harmony with God, and thus, we are born to live in harmony with God. This harmony is being holy in God.

The process of our holiness will always be ongoing. The process will be a second-by-second thing, a minute-by-minute thing, an hour-by-hour thing, and a day-by-day thing. From the moment that Adam and Eve committed the first sin, it broke that harmony with God. Sin is in our lives and the world. It's disrupting the harmony. Until we submit ourselves fully to God every day, then sin will be a constant shadow in our hearts, and holiness will slip right through our fingers every time. With great urgency, Paul warns us that our body, our lives, and our hearts are God's temple, "Don't you know that you yourselves are God's temple and that God's Spirit dwells in your midst" (1 Corinthians 3:16, NIV)? So, when we constantly sin, the holiness of God becomes disrupted, and we start to become desensitized to the Holy Spirit's proddings.

When Jesus walked this earth, He was the living embodiment of holiness, but when He was crucified, He promised us an Advocate, a friend, the Holy Spirit. This same Holy Spirit descends upon us like a dove. The Holy Spirit keeps us in tune with God. When we sin, the Holy Spirit will convict us. When we worship God, the Holy Spirit will envelop us with love and holiness. The Holy Spirit is our guide to living holy. Submitting ourselves, becoming in tune with, and opening our hearts to the Holy Spirit will guide us to be more God-like. No longer does brokenness affect our hearts the way it did. Instead, the Holy Spirit is indwelling in our hearts, assuring us to remain holy by giving over all our hearts and all our souls.

To grow and become more holy, we must go through trials. Since brokenness is the major theme throughout this book, and we are on our last stage of becoming whole again, we can understand more easily how our trials help us grow and become more holy. The trials you have gone through in overcoming your brokenness have instilled in you an endurance you never knew you had and perseverance that surpasses the most daunting tribulations. Without you realizing it, as you have endured and persevered, you have become closer to God. Becoming more holy in Him. Second Peter 1:5–8 says,

> Make every effort to add to your faith goodness; and to goodness, knowledge; and to knowledge, self-control; and to self-control, perseverance; and to perseverance, godliness; and to godliness, mutual affection; and to mutual affection, love. For if you possess these qualities in increasing measure, they will keep you from being ineffective and unproductive in your knowledge of our Lord Jesus Christ.

> 2 Peter 1:5–8 (NIV)

If we cave into the pressure, worry, pride, unforgiveness, hate, and anger of our broken heart, then we will become ineffective and unproductive for Jesus as it says in 2 Peter 1:5–8. A holy heart will become non-existent if we don't endure and persevere. We must persevere for the sake of our hearts. A holy heart is what we need to get to the forever heart, and a forever heart is what we need for living eternally. Persevering brings glory to God amid our trials, persevering overcomes all the odds, and persevering turns the broken heart into a holy heart.

Becoming sanctified in the Lord is a war between light and dark. A spiritual war ensues, God versus Satan. And we are in the midst of the war. During this war, we are commanded by God to clothe ourselves with Jesus and resist the urge to obey the passions of the flesh. Our armor in securing holiness during the war is light (see Romans 3:12). This light is visible to the spiritual world and invisible to the eyes that choose to see fleshly. It's God's light. God's light is so bright that the shadows cower and flee in its presence. This same light is within us. It's within us when we sanctify ourselves in Christ. He becomes our light in a darkened world. "The light shines in the darkness, and the darkness has not overcome it" (John 1:5, NIV).

A holy heart shaped by the trials we face leads to a redeemed heart. The heart will not be labeled as broken anymore. Once you choose to sanctify yourself, brokenness is washed away along with the other sins that kept you chained. With the Holy Spirit's leading, you are redeemed from the power of your brokenness. The life you once led as a broken person with a broken heart is no more. Now, your life is renewed, renewed by the sacrificial blood of Jesus. Renewed because He rose from the grave. This is what the Apostle Paul said,

> We were therefore buried with him through baptism into death in order that, just as Christ was raised from the dead through the glory of the Father, we too may live a new life. For if we have been united with him in a death like his, we will certainly also be united with him in a resurrection like his.

Romans 6:4–5 (NIV)

We were dead in our old life. Our old way of thinking. Our old brokenness. But when Jesus died for us and when we became holy in Him, united with Him, we became alive again. We became life. We became redeemed. He set us free from all of our sins, including our brokenness. We only have to grasp His redemption.

Understand this: God has been redeeming His people from the beginning. From Joseph to Moses and from David to Daniel, He is the Redeemer. David even described God as the Redeemer in one of his psalms. "Praise the LORD, my soul, and forget not all his benefits—who forgives all your sins and heals all your diseases, who redeems your life from the pit and crowns you with love and compassion" (Psalm 103:2–4, NIV). If God was redeeming His people without the sacrificial blood of Jesus, then think of how powerful His redemption is with the sacrificial blood of Jesus. Our redemption is forever.

The redemption of our hearts is the epitome of our forever heart. With the confidence, love, forgiveness, humility, righteousness, holiness, and redemption of God, let us rejoice in a heart that is made whole. Let us rejoice in a heart that embodies the Almighty God. Let us rejoice of the magnificent forever heart.

ENDNOTES

1. James Strong, *The New Strong's Expanded Exhaustive Concordance of the Bible* (Nashville: Thomas Nelson, 2010), 139

2. "Gullain-Barre Syndrome," Mayo Clinic, accessed July 23rd, 2021

3. "Guillain-Barré Syndrome Fact Sheet," National Institute of Neurological Disorders and Stroke, accessed March 16th, 2021

4. "Peace, "Merriam Webster's Dictionary, accessed October 28th, 2021

5. Ryken et al., *Dictionary of Biblical Imagery* (Illinois: Inter-Varsity Press, 1998), 792

6. "Forgive," Merriam Webster's Dictionary, accessed October 28th, 2021

7. James Strong, *The New Strong's Expanded Exhaustive Concordance of the Bible* (Nashville: Thomas Nelson, 2010), 208

8. James Strong, *The New Strong's Expanded Exhaustive Concordance of the Bible* (Nashville: Thomas Nelson, 2010), 238

9. James Strong, *The New Strong's Expanded Exhaustive Concordance of the Bible* (Nashville: Thomas Nelson, 2010), 40

10. James Strong, *The New Strong's Expanded Exhaustive Concordance of the Bible* (Nashville: Thomas Nelson, 2010), 92

11. "Firm," Merriam Webster's Dictionary, accessed October 28th, 2021

12. "How the Heart Works," WebMD, accessed October 24th, 2020

13. Ryken et al., *Dictionary of Biblical Imagery* (Illinois: Inter-Varsity Press, 1998), 262

14. "Confidence," Merriam Webster's Dictionary, accessed October 28th, 2021

15. Brand et al., *Holman Illustrated Bible Dictionary* (Nashville, Tennessee: B&H Publishing Group, 2015), 765

16. Brand et al., *Holman Illustrated Bible Dictionary* (Nashville, Tennessee: B&H Publishing Group, 2015), 1339

17. "Righteousness," Merriam Webster's Dictionary, accessed October 28th, 2021

18. Ryken et al., *Dictionary of Biblical Imagery* (Illinois: Inter-Varsity Press, 1998), 758

BIBLIOGRAPHY

Brand, Chad, Eric Mitchell, eds. *Holman Illustrated Bible Dictionary*. Nashville, Tennessee: B&H Publishing Group, 2015.

Mayo Clinic. "Gullain-Barre Syndrome." Mayo Clinic. Accessed July 23rd, 2021. https://www.mayoclinic.org/diseases-conditions/guillain-barre-syndrome/symptoms-causes/syc-20362793

Merriam-Webster Dictionary. "Confidence." Merriam-Webster Dictionary. Accessed October 28th, 2021. https://www.merriam-webster.com/dictionary/confidence

Merriam-Webster Dictionary. "Firm." Merriam-Webster Dictionary. Accessed October 28th, 2021. https://www.merriam-webster.com/dictionary/firm

Merriam-Webster Dictionary. "Forgive." Merriam-Webster Dictionary. Accessed October 28th, 2021. https://www.merriam-webster.com/dictionary/forgive

Merriam-Webster Dictionary. "Peace." Merriam-Webster Dictionary. Accessed October 28th, 2021. https://www.merriam-webster.com/thesaurus/peace

Merriam-Webster Dictionary. "Righteousness." Merriam-Webster Dictionary. Accessed October 28th, 2021. https://www.merriam-webster.com/dictionary/righteousness

National Institute on Neurological Disorders and Stroke. "Gul-lain-Barré Syndrome Fact Sheet." National Institute on Neurological Disorders and Stroke. Accessed March 16th, 2021. https://www.ninds.nih.gov/Disorders/Patient-Care-giver-Education/Fact-Sheets/Guillain-Barr%C3%A9-Syn-drome-Fact-Sheet

Ryken, Leland, James C. Wilhoit, and Tremper Longman, eds. *Dictionary of Biblical Imagery*. Downers Grove, Illinois: InterVarsity Press, 1998.

Strong, James. *The New Strong's Expanded Exhaustive Concordance of the Bible*. Nashville: Thomas Nelson, 2010.

WebMD. "How the Heart Works." WebMD. Accessed August 24th, 2020. https://www.webmd.com/heart-disease/guide/how-heart-works

About the Author

Kaela Saner was born and raised in the Northern Kentucky area, just outside of Cincinnati, Ohio. Kaela considers her relationship with Jesus Christ and her family to be the most important to her. She has had to adapt and work through many situations in her life, from living in Alaska for six months to moving to Washington state for a few years and then back to Kentucky, as well as navigating the challenges that come with collegiate athletics. If Kaela is not spending time with friends and family, you can almost always find her studying the Word of God or reading the Word of God.